MUTANT SEX PARTY

ALSO BY ED MACDONALD
Spat the Dummy (novel)

MUTANT SEX PARTY

& OTHER PLAYS

BY ED MACDONALD

ANVIL PRESS | VANCOUVER | TWENTY-TWELVE

Copyright © 2012 by Ed Macdonald

Anvil Press Publishers Inc.
P.O. Box 3008, Main Post Office
Vancouver, B.C. V6B 3X5 Canada
www.anvilpress.com

All rights reserved. No part of this book may be reproduced by any means without the prior written permission of the publisher, with the exception of brief passages in reviews. Any request for photocopying or other reprographic copying of any part of this book must be directed in writing to ACCESS: The Canadian Copyright Licensing Agency, One Yonge Street, Suite 800, Toronto, Ontario, Canada, M5E 1E5.

LIBRARY AND ARCHIVES CANADA CATALOGUING IN PUBLICATION

Macdonald, Ed
    Mutant sex party / Ed Macdonald.

Plays.
ISBN 978-1-897535-93-6

    I. Title.

PS8625.D628M87 2012   C812'.6   C2012-901160-6

Anvil Performance Series ISSN 1188-0872; no. 8

Printed and bound in Canada
Cover design by Typesmith Design
Interior design by HeimatHouse
Author photo by Sabrina Reeves
Cover: Tom Demenkoff and Erik Van Wyck in The Drilling Company (NY) production.

Represented in Canada by the Literary Press Group
Distributed by the University of Toronto Press

The publisher gratefully acknowledges the financial assistance of the Canada Council for the Arts, the Canada Book Fund, and the Province of British Columbia through the B.C. Arts Council and the Book Publishing Tax Credit.

CONTENTS

6

RAQs (Rarely Asked Questions):
In Conversation with Ed Macdonald

THE PLAYS

9

Mutant Sex Party

77

Gemini

103

Dead Meat

117

Smoke and Blood

155

The Escape Artist

167

The Returns

RAQs (Rarely Asked Questions)

In Conversation with Ed Macdonald (aka Edward Manning)

Why Do You Have Two Names?

I have three, actually. I'm not entirely sure as to the why of it. Years ago, I decided to use my middle name as a surname when I was writing plays. I suppose that I thought it sounded like a serious playwright's name. Also, I felt that the name Macdonald had a negative connotation due to the existence of an insanely successful fast food franchise. I don't want to say which one. Anyway, Manning is my middle name and that's why I used it. I don't anymore. My third name is a whole other story. I'm not even sure how to spell it.

When Did This Get So Out Of Hand?

When I was sixteen years old, I sat in the James McConnell Memorial Library in Sydney, Nova Scotia and read Samuel Beckett's *Waiting for Godot*. When I finished it I knew, with reassuring certainty, that everything had changed. The only other time I had experienced the same sensation was four years earlier when I heard *Never Mind the Bullocks, Here's the Sex Pistols*.

Hilarious, inexplicable and purgatorial, *Godot* is rife with horrifying truths. I used Beckett's masterpiece as a licence to dismiss convention and to ignore all expectations. A play, he demonstrated, did not have to be sensible or formal or logical.

I started doing one-act plays at The Boardmore Playhouse at Cape Breton University. It was a great time and place for young upstarts and sulking hipsters. Elizabeth and Harry Boardmore had created a festival that enthusiastically encouraged new writers. We had the opportunity to learn by doing and we were given a lot of leeway. The only thing they would not let me have on the stage was fire. I was delighted to within an inch of my life.

Later, in my twenties, I gave up theatre for a while and landed a few writing and acting gigs in television. Nothing on screen can ever have the same impact as something live on a stage, though, so I keep coming back.

But, Why?

Because. Theatre is inherently more important than any other form because it takes us to the root of all human experience: people in darkness, gathered around a light to hear a story. And, ultimately, stories define us and determine our fate. No matter how compelling the narrative projected on it, the screen is dead. The stage is alive. There's more risk and higher expectations because it happens right in front of us.

What's The Deal With These Plays?
Well, let's see. *Mutant Sex Party*. The first version was a short written for a Drilling Company show in New York. Erik Van Wyck and Tom Demenkoff were spectacular in it and that first production inspired the longer version herein. Erik and Tom returned for the second, full-length production in June of 2005 and they were pitch perfect in it. It was written during the reign of beloved simpleton, George W. Bush, and is, ultimately, an homage to the mating ball of vampires that would come to be known as the "one percent."

Then there's *Gemini*. Victor Syperek owns a bar in Halifax, Nova Scotia, called The Economy Shoe Shop. One summer he had a reading series and asked me to swing by and harass his patrons with my subtle, almost imperceptible charm. I read a strange, fragmented, untitled monologue that appealed to an actor friend named Kenneth-Wilson Harrington, or as I call him, Kenny. He thought that there was a play in it, I agreed and what I read that day became the core of *Gemini*. The first production was directed by Christian Murray and ran at the Neptune Theatre second stage in Halifax, Nova Scotia. The second production, also starring Kenny, was directed by David Kennedy and happened off-Broadway in 2001. It was later remounted for a run at PSNBC, a showcase space run by NBC.

Dead Meat is a love story, obviously. It's a short written for another Drilling Company show. It's about impatience, ambivalence, boredom, love, hate, fear, trees, meat theft and running. *Smoke and Blood* grew out of a play called *Titus Lucretius Carus* which was nominated for Best Script at the New York Innovative Theater Awards. So, there. This version takes place during two distinctly different parties: one in 55 B.C. and one that happened last night. It's about the end of Titus's life, about the gods and their stubborn refusal to exist. *The Escape Artist* is another love story. I've lost count of how many versions there are of this one. It's about the need to connect and the fear of what that connection might imply. Also, it has a whale. *The Returns* was originally called *Erratica* and appeared at the West 78th Street Theater Lab in Manhattan. It is a one-man show and will never end; a sliver of an eternity "on tour."

Anything Else?
Yes. Though some of the characters in these plays are age and gender specific, race has no relevance when it comes to casting.

What Else?
I'm grateful to Elizabeth and Harry Boardmore, Gary Walsh, Maynard Morrison, Bette MacDonald, Ron Jenkins, Hamilton Clancy and the countless actors, directors, technicians and designers with whom I have had the privilege of working. Thanks, everybody!

MUTANT SEX PARTY

MUTANT SEX PARTY

Scene One:

Muted lights on a hotel suite.

Clay wears jeans and combat boots. His T-shirt is on the floor. He's in his mid-twenties.

John is in his forties. He's a little drunk, tired. He sits on the floor, in a rumpled suit, rubbing his forehead.

Clay's anger is unconvincing. He approaches John.

CLAY: (*drill sergeant*) You're a greasy fuckin' piece of shit!

JOHN: (*for the last time*) No.

CLAY: Ya dirty fuckin' prick!

JOHN: I mean, that's not it.

CLAY: Well, what then?

JOHN: You have to tell me things. Specific things — that I've done.

CLAY: I can't remember all that shit, man.

JOHN: You know. Everybody knows.

CLAY: You're sure you don't want a blow job? Most people just want a blow job, you know. It's not without its charms.

JOHN: You have to focus your hatred — and tell me.

CLAY: I don't hate you, baby.

JOHN: Don't call — part of you does. A big part, probably. You can pretend the rest.

CLAY: You make too many assumptions. Now, what do you really want? Cuz I can't be playin' *Days of Our Lives* with ya all night, Skip.

JOHN: Skip?

CLAY: Well, what's your name?

JOHN: You know my name.

CLAY: Is it Skippy?

JOHN: Start over.

CLAY: (*Huh?*) What's that?

JOHN: Walk over there and then come back and — and you have to shred me. Don't hold anything back. But don't touch me, either.

Clay produces something between a scoff and a sigh. After a beat, he takes a few steps away from John.

JOHN: Ja hear me?

CLAY: I hear ya.

Pause. Clay thinks. He suddenly approaches John, enraged.

CLAY: OK, you fuckin' bag of rat shit, I'm gonna kick your fuckin' head off!

JOHN: (*calmly*) You're not even trying.

CLAY: You're high, aren't ya?

JOHN: Look — you have to focus every violent impulse you have ever had, every —

CLAY: I'm just not angry, I guess.

JOHN: Shut up and listen!

John stands.

CLAY: You're baked. And you know that shit's bad for you.

JOHN: Clay!

CLAY: (*aping him*) What!

JOHN: Listen.

John pauses, is about to speak.

CLAY: (*calmly*) How often you gettin' high? Everyday, maybe?

John sighs.

CLAY: (*nodding*) What's that costing the taxpayers?

JOHN: Have you started over? Is this a new approach?

CLAY: Do you like it?

JOHN: No. It has to be more extreme and not so — general. More venom. You have to yell.

CLAY: This is *sooo* —

JOHN: It has to be pure hate.

CLAY: —stupid.

JOHN: Pure fucking hatred. And you have to remind me of everything I've done, or it doesn't work.

CLAY: I don't know what you —

JOHN: Just say what the average asshole on the street would say I did. Bring it hard and I'll double your money.

CLAY: You're a sick fuck, John.

JOHN: Don't start yet.

CLAY: I didn't. I'm just sayin' you're a sick fuck.

JOHN: Look... do it the way I want, OK? I have to give that crap speech in two hours.

Pause. Clay regards John, coldly, for a moment.

CLAY: Look, you don't want me. I don't know dick about squat, so...

JOHN: (*bellows*) DO YOU WANT MY FUCKING MONEY OR NOT?

Silence. Clay regards John, seriously. John stares at him.

CLAY: OK, John... here it is... your tedious problem — in a nutshell — is that you have no self-respect.

JOHN: Say... what I've done.

CLAY: And because you have no self-respect, you're incapable of having respect for other people — and that's why they all call you "Prick" or "Big Dirty Prick."

JOHN: That hurt my feelings.

CLAY: See, where normal people want respect, you want fear. Cuz that's what drives you, Bonzo.

JOHN: You're a lazy piece of shit.

CLAY: Fear is ignorance, John. You cling to your ignorance cuz it's what you know best, but it won't protect you. The world seeps in.

JOHN: I'm not paying for this, I hope you know.

CLAY: You keep running — with your eyes shut tight. Afraid all the time because you think everybody's dangerous. You believe things — and that warps your perception of —

JOHN: If you're not going to play, just get the fuck out.

CLAY: Don't bother butchering that speech. You're so fucking... dead inside that you can't even say the words anymore. Every time you open that glory hole of a mouth — you just...you sound out the syllables — like a...a —

JOHN: I don't think I need notes from you.

CLAY: ...drunk robot.

JOHN: And don't think you've wormed your way into anything permanent, boy. You're a snack. Now, either play right or get the fuck out.

John begins to straighten himself out. He checks himself in a mirror. Clay becomes slightly menacing, standing a little too close to John.

CLAY: It's not enough to whack-off to your rap sheet, Butch. You're a leech. You need blood.

JOHN: You can go now.

CLAY: Nothing happened to you. You didn't have a traumatic experience. You weren't forced into it. You chose this, my friend.

JOHN: Let's have your voice box out for your birthday, 'K?

CLAY: See, it's not what you do. I don't care that you're on the take. Who isn't? I don't care that you and your boys stole the election. Doesn't matter who wins.

JOHN: What's wrong with you?

CLAY: No matter which one of you greasy old fucks gets to read the speeches, it's nothing to the rest of us.

JOHN: Whatever kind of drugs you're —

CLAY: It's not that you refuse to clean up that — that outrageous tonnage of chemical shit that poisons the water where I lived.

JOHN: (*puzzled*) What?

CLAY: It's not that you're a liar and a fraud and a throwback to the Stone Age with all the morals of a rabid jackal. That's what we expect from your kind. The birds sing, the dogs bark and you suck. That's the way folks want it.

JOHN: What chemicals poison what water?

CLAY: The issue — what quietly sickens us Norms, Johnny — is that you still believe that mutating into this creature you've become was some kind of accomplishment. As if your fuckedupness is legitimate somehow and rational. You haven't tricked them, Johnny. Johnny! You're not fooling them. You're not fooling them. They're just playing along cuz they're scared. And lazy. Flitting from screen to screen, dreaming.

JOHN: Do you know how easy it would be for me to make you disappear?

CLAY: Yes... but you won't... cuz I'm probably one of the few people you've ever gotten to know in your whole, stupid, parody of a life.

JOHN: You think so?

CLAY: I do. And listen to me, Skip. I'm not judging you. These are just casual observations I'm making. I actually respect you. I do. Cuz to reach this lofty plain — upon which you are currently rotting — you've had to suck a great many more cocks than I, Sir. And for that, I salute you.

JOHN: Go while you still can, Clay.

CLAY: I'm just sayin', for your own good, it's not natural to be what you are.

JOHN: Get out!

CLAY: Rich or poor, Johnny, young or old, you're all the same dismal, desperate guy. Nature — the real world — doesn't need you for anything. You're built on made-up shit. As soon as the TV is done with you, everything goes back to how it was before you snowed them.

JOHN: Get out... now!

Pause. Clay stares.

CLAY: Make me.

Pause. John scoffs.

JOHN: Don't get tough.

Pause. Clay stares at John.

CLAY: (*quietly*) What if I did?

Pause. John sobers a little.

JOHN: Billy's parked downstairs...he'll come up if I'm late.

CLAY: So?

JOHN: He's not just a driver, you know. He can break your neck.

Clay shoves John. John stumbles a bit.

JOHN: I'm telling you, Kid —

CLAY: Are ya scared, Skip?

JOHN: Listen to me —

Clay, suddenly, has John in a headlock. John struggles. Clay punches John, hard, in the stomach.

CLAY: (*calmly*) You want to get punished for the shit you've done?

JOHN: No!

Clay releases John, throwing him to the floor where he curls into a fetal position, then gradually...

JOHN: No.

CLAY: Not for real.

JOHN: You're in serious trouble, now.

Clay kicks John in the stomach and walks away. John coughs and groans. Clay watches him, arms folded. Silence.

CLAY: To give you the punishment you deserve I'd have to kill you... Now, I'd be doing the world a favour... but I'd be doing it your way... and even I have too much self-respect for that.

Pause. John looks up at Clay.

JOHN: If this is a new game, I really don't like it.

Pause. Clay crouches about a foot from John.

CLAY: You're boring. You bore me... you primitive fuck.

Pause. Clay watches John. His disgust deepens.

JOHN: (*sitting up, staying calm*) I'll pay you anyway... and you can have the room for the rest of the night — if you want.

CLAY: (*standing*) I can have anything, John... I know things about you they wouldn't believe in jail.

Pause. The threat takes the edge off John's fear.

JOHN: That's a dangerous move, Clay.

Pause. They consider each other.

CLAY: (*flatly*) Is it?

Pause. John slows his breathing, staying calm.

JOHN: I'll pretend that was just a new thing...you were trying out...and we'll forget it.

Pause. John considers Clay. John extends a hand.

JOHN: Help me up. (*Pause. Clay considers John's hand.*) Come on.

Finally, Clay pulls John to his feet. He cradles the back of John's head, tenderly, as though he is going to kiss him. John is guarded. Clay slaps him, hard. He then turns John's face toward his own.

CLAY: I've always wanted to do that.

Pause. Clay strokes John's cheek, gently, chuckling softly.

CLAY: Isn't really what you had in mind, is it?

Pause. John manages to stay calm.

JOHN: (*quietly*) No.

CLAY: No...and I'm a little smarter than you thought, maybe... little stronger...full of surprises...you make a lot of stupid assumptions, baby.

Clay shoves John's face away. John backs off. Clay approaches, steadily.

CLAY: You chose this.

JOHN: Stop it, now.

CLAY: It's not any system or tradition or anybody's sad old fucking ideas turning everything to shit. It's just you. It's you. And the media whores. (*Clay shoves John. John moves away.*) Scurrying where normal people walk.

JOHN: Listen to me.

Clay shoves John. John moves away.

CLAY: No fun being King, is it, John? That only means you have to run faster, right? Yeah. The truth is always nipping at your heels — filling the space you just left. Catching up.

JOHN: Now you listen to me. I'm sure that —

CLAY: I'm not done! You shut the fuck up!... You're convinced. You're so in it, you're blind. But lately... You feel the seams pulling apart... look at what you are, now. Look at it... what the fuck are you doing here — with me? Your wife can't throw a punch, *what*? Don't get me wrong, I wouldn't fuck with her.

Pause. Clay approaches John until they are eye to eye.

CLAY: What is it her family makes? Insecticide, is it? I bet she used to stink of it — back when you were dating. I bet she still does. I bet there's nothing from the outside living in your house.

JOHN: Look. I just want to go —

CLAY: You just want what? What now?... Take this free advice — from my heart to yours. Pick a rooftop, mutherfucker. And spread your wings. You're a relic. And you could at least go back to hell in a way that would give us all a little laugh. Okay? Bleed your own blood for a change. Redeem yourself.

Silence. John steps back, cautiously. Slowly, he produces a roll of cash, cautiously offers it to Clay.

JOHN: That's more than double.

Clay stares. Pause. John slowly places the cash on the floor, near Clay's feet. He straightens, wary of Clay.

JOHN: I'm going... you can have the room... but I have to go.

Pause. John waits for a response. Clay stares, hands at his sides. Finally, John turns and starts out. Suddenly, Clay pounces, throwing John to the floor. John lands on his side, his back to us. Clay kicks him in the stomach, twice. John curls up a little. Clay jumps down, straddling him. Using both hands, Clay presses John's head into the floor. John screams, squirms.

CLAY: Being a coward makes you evil, Skip. And being evil makes you small. You're small — and easy to kill.

JOHN: (*screams unintelligibly*) Stop!

CLAY: And even though I can't extinguish you, the way I should, I can put you halfway there. Right? Am I right?

John cries out. Clay takes a few deep breaths. Silence. Finally, he releases John, stands and spits on him. After a beat, he finds his shirt, puts it on.

John folds, gasps a little as he ejaculates. Clay goes to the money, counts it. John sighs heavily, twice, perfectly satiated. When Clay is done counting:

JOHN: Careful with the face, will you?

CLAY: (*pocketing the money*) Sorry.

Clay grabs his jacket, starts out.

JOHN: Tell Billy I need a change of clothes. And get me some wine.

CLAY: Yeah.

JOHN: And come right back. You're not hanging around that club all night.

CLAY: (*off, mumbles*) Yeah, yeah.

Exit Clay.

Contented, John lies back, sighs. He extends his arms, stretching. SFX: A cell phone rings.

JOHN: (*mutters*) Oh, for fuck —

John goes to the phone, answers it with his back to us.

Yeah... what?... Slow down... what are you telling me?

After a beat, he takes the phone from his ear.

JOHN: FUCK!

Blackout.

Scene Two:

A quick flurry of flashbulbs precedes the light downstage. John walks into it, self-assured, smiling. He speaks with sincere warmth and humility, addressing the scrum like it is a crowd of old friends.

JOHN: No, listen, Lynnette and I are confident that we will be vindicated and that this mess will be behind us and — we will prevail. Look, there is a price — let me say this, Kevin, there is a price to pay when you choose to make the public service your life. My wife and I have been targeted by a politically motivated witch hunt that...

He looks to the left, listens for a second, responds to the unheard question.

JOHN: Yes, Todd Burns is a — an acquaintance of ours...yes, but are we guilty by association? Keep in mind neither Lynnette nor I have been charged with any wrongdoing. And the reason we haven't is because there has been no insider trading, no... backroom deals, nothing. It's pure fiction. Pure invention on the part of the liberal media. And, as I say, we fully expect to have this matter behind us — as soon as the investigation — or, *inquiry*, rather — is over.

He points to another reporter. Short pause.

JOHN: Lynnette's great. She isn't worried in the least because she knows, and God knows, that we haven't done anything wrong. She's in bed with a bit of a head cold today, so I'm going to attempt to make chicken soup when I get home. That could be a lot more newsworthy. If you guys want a real disaster story, it'll be in our kitchen later tonight.

SFX: TV sit-com laugh.

John smiles at the laughing group of reporters. It's over. He gives a small wave as he exits in another flurry of camera flashes.

SFX: TV sit-com laugh into applause.

Scene Three:

Clay is on the bed.

CLAY: You worry too much, Johnny. This will all blow over — like a cloud of toxic gas. Everything blows over, eventually.

John enters in a fresh shirt, tying his tie. He goes to the unseen mirror and checks his eyes. He is clearly afraid.

CLAY: Here, Skip.

JOHN: Go to the other room.

CLAY: I got your wine.

He removes cocaine, holds it up.

CLAY: It's good, too.

JOHN: (*whispers*) Aw, fuck.

John runs off, to the bathroom. We hear John vomit.

CLAY: Now, Hon, I don't like the sound of that cough one bit.

JOHN: (*between heaves*) Get the fuck out of here!

CLAY: Listen to me, Skip. You've got, what, twenty lawyers now? A shitload of money and a can-do spirit. There's no way they can make this stick and you know it!

John groans, catching his breath, still deeply nauseated.

CLAY: So, the minute you wiggle off the hook, we'll have a big party and forget all about it. Anyway, according to my calendar, tomorrow is the first day of Spring, so I have to shake it up.

John wretches.

CLAY: And you know me, baby — I am the Celebration Alpha and Omega. All parties begin and end exactly where I'm standing.

John wretches.

CLAY: And if you're really good, I'll get you so high your brain will slosh around your skull like water in a jug on a warm day in June. We'll fuck like it's four years ago and have a nice pasta.

John groans, exhausted.

CLAY: Then, the next day, we'll get the guitars out and play some folk songs together. A little Woody, a little Neil. All those protest songs you love so much.

John enters, sweating, wiping his face with a towel.

CLAY: Gettin' hungry?

JOHN: Go. Now.

Clay goes to John. He begins to twist his torso from side to side as he pokes at John, mechanically, alternating hands.

CLAY: Aw, you'll see, Skip. It'll all work out swell. Well, something will happen, anyway. And something's better than nothing. Am I right? Am I right?...Am I right?

John slaps Clay's hand away, regards Clay for a moment.

JOHN: Look... this is a lot more serious than you seem to realize. I'm...

CLAY: What? What's on your mind, L'il Joe?

Pause. John closes his eyes and has a brief, waking dream. His head moves slightly, his mouth twitches. He opens his eyes, empties his lungs.

John stares at Clay for a moment.

CLAY: What?

JOHN: Look... it's getting obvious that we've come to the end of the road... I can't have you around right now. Okay? Don't make it ugly. Just get your stuff and go... Billy will get you a plane ticket to wherever you want.

CLAY: Business class?

JOHN: Don't ever try to contact me... I like you. But if you ever talk to anyone about me — if you even speak my name to anyone... well... you understand.

Pause. Clay stares at John. John stands, removes his cash, puts it on the bed.

JOHN Have a good life... I mean that.

Exit John.

Pause.

Clay considers the money. Finally, he stands, puts on his boots. He looks toward John's exit for a moment.

Scene Four:

Dim light on the bed. John enters, weary and a little drunk. He begins to undress slowly, eventually gives up and hugs the bed. Unable to get comfortable, he sits up, throws his shirt, falls on his back and sighs deeply. Silence. Clay leaps up from beside the bed, pounces on John and begins violently choking him. John struggles, limbs flailing. Clay is very drunk.

CLAY: You don't fucking use me! You understand that? I want that to be the last thing you hear, motherfucker! You — don't — fucking — use — ME!

Gradually, John's struggle weakens until he falls back lifeless. Clay releases him. He catches his breath. He looks at John's face, recoils.

Clay takes a few unconscious, backward steps away from the bed. Pause.

CLAY: (*quietly*) John?

Pause. Clay approaches John.

CLAY: John?

Pause. Dread rises in Clay.

CLAY: (*whispers*) Oh, fuck...oh, fuck.

He goes to John, listens to his heart. He stands, considers him. He exhales, sharply as the reality of it hits him. Finally, he goes to the phone, dials.

CLAY: Billy...shut up...shut up and listen. Listen to me...

Something happened... something... I didn't mean to do it.

John gasps and is physically jolted as though breath is being forced into him. Clay jumps, startled. John moves a little. Clay watches him for a moment.

CLAY: Billy? Never mind. No, we're just fuckin' around.

Clay hangs up the phone, turns and walks away from the bed. He drops his head, relieved. Silence.

John sits up, breathing hard, coughing. He calms his breath, watches Clay for a moment. He scrambles for the phone, pulls it off the night table. Seeing this, Clay rushes to John and grabs the phone out of his hand. John recoils.

JOHN: Don't...

Clay hangs up the phone. Pause. He regards John.

CLAY: I'm sorry... I'm sorry... I'm all... fucked up.

Pause. Clay is at a loss.

CLAY: You okay?

Pause. Clay is shaken.

CLAY: I don't know what I was thinking... I swear, I was just... I'm sorry.

Pause. John moves away from Clay.

JOHN: I'm... I better go home.

CLAY: No.

JOHN: I should...I should be seen leaving the house in the morning.

CLAY: Listen...you have to stay. Just...see...you took a lot of time from me...and given my family history and whatnot, I might not have that much left...so every minute matters to me...there's no spare time.

Pause. John watches Clay.

JOHN: (*quietly*) Sure.

Pause. Clay regards John.

CLAY: Okay...go back to sleep.

JOHN: What?

CLAY: Lie down and go to sleep.

Pause. John regards Clay.

JOHN: I think I'm up for a while.

CLAY: Lie down.

Keeping his eyes on Clay, John reclines against the pillows on the far side of the bed. Silence. Clay watches him. John stares into space.

CLAY: You were dead.

Silence. Clay watches John.

CLAY: John?

Pause. John stares into space.

CLAY: You were dead.

JOHN: I know.

Silence. Clay watches John as the lights bleed out.

SFX: A slightly slowed down recording of a steady intake of breath.

Blackout.

Scene Five:

SFX: The inhalation sound gets steadily louder until it becomes a thunderous roar.

The sound stops suddenly and morning lights snap on over the bed.

John and Clay stand next to it. John slaps Clay.

CLAY: I was drunk! I'm sorry. I was playing Revenge Killing.

John goes to the mirror, examines his neck.

JOHN: Then why didn't you use the tie? The silk tie! I've got your fucking paw marks all over my neck now. Jesus Christ! I thought you were supposed to be smart.

CLAY: I was upset for real, maybe.

JOHN: Maybe? You nearly fucking —

Pause. John ties his tie.

CLAY: Not nearly. I did...I did...look...I can't do this full-time thing anymore. I can't be cooped up in here like this...ja hear me?

Suddenly overcome, John pulls the tie off and avoids tears by getting mad.

JOHN: Fuck! Fuck!

He drops the tie, can't hold it together. He sobs. Pause. Clay approaches, unsure of what to do.

CLAY: What now?

JOHN: They're... they're going to find us guilty.

CLAY: Naw, look, that inquiry won't even have a decision for a long time yet.

JOHN: It's Friday!

CLAY: Oh.

JOHN: Aw, christ.

Pause. John gradually recovers.

JOHN: They'll bury me. They've been waiting for something like this.

CLAY: Oh, come on.

JOHN: There's blood in the water.

CLAY: The lawyers can weasel you out of this. They always do. Besides, if they toss you out, you just write a book and then run the next time.

John regards Clay, laughs, genuinely amused. He laughs, quietly, for a long time.

CLAY: What?... What?

JOHN: You're such a little prick.

CLAY: You can run again.

JOHN: Fucking —

CLAY: It only takes one cleverly written speech.

Clay opens his arms and tilts his head, as if to say, "Here I am."

CLAY: You must know that by now. You just get Chris to raise some cash, you get on TV with those eyebrows raised with that *Who, me?* kind of expression you use. With my words dribbling out of you, they'll put you right back at the head of the table. You're useful. Trust me, I know how you guys operate.

JOHN: (*whispers*) Christ.

CLAY: Oh, you'll see, Johnny. This is just a bump in the road. A small gash in an otherwise healthy body.

Clay dances a little to the house music in his head.

CLAY: We're gonna have fun!

Clay does the ancient falsetto disco double whoop, pumping his hands in the air, in time with it.

JOHN: Shut up, all right?

Clay stops dancing. Silence. John goes to the bed to get his suit jacket, puts it on. He ignores Clay who watches him closely.

CLAY: I could tell you were gone... for a few seconds, anyway, you were dead... that's pretty fucked up, Skip. I called Billy and everything.

JOHN: You called Billy?

CLAY: Yeah. To like, get help. I told him to call an ambulance but then you came back... you were dead... it has to mean something to you.

Pause. John watches him for a moment.

JOHN: Does it?

CLAY: It's big.

Pause. John considers Clay for moment, regains his usual posture.

JOHN: I'm not done until about eleven tonight. Don't go out and don't go to sleep. (*starting out*) I'm calling The Agency.

CLAY: Aw, for fucksake!

JOHN: Take a shower.

Exit John.

Clay watches where he has gone.

Scene Six:

John is drunk, sitting on the bed. He freshens his drink. There's a knock. He exits, returns followed by Clay. Clay is shy and nervous.

JOHN: Come in. Make yourself... what's your name?

CLAY: Clay.

JOHN: What?

CLAY: My name is Clay.

JOHN: All right. My name's Mud.

John chuckles. Clay stares, not getting it.

CLAY: They told me to get the money up front.

JOHN: You get your clothes off and then we'll decide what you're worth. How about that?

CLAY: It's two hundred. I need the money up front.

Pause. John watches him.

JOHN: You seem nervous... Is it me? Are you nervous about meeting me? I suppose I look different in person.

Pause. Clay watches him.

CLAY: The Agency says get the money first.

JOHN: You give me your pants and I'll give you the money.

Clay sighs. He goes down on one knee to untie his boot.

JOHN: You want a drink, Mr. Clay?

CLAY: I don't drink.

JOHN: Good for you... you're new at this, aren't you?

CLAY: Yeah.

JOHN: Good.

Clay takes off his pants, hands them to John.

JOHN: I have no time for people who are tired of their work.

CLAY: Put the money in the pocket. It's two hundred. Three, if I stay the night.

Pause. John tosses the pants.

JOHN: What have you done?

Pause. Clay is genuinely unsure of how this goes.

CLAY: What's that?

JOHN: What have you done — that put you here? In such a specialized line of work.

CLAY: What would you like it to be?

JOHN: Something pathetic.

CLAY: I'm a junky with a pregnant junky girlfriend and I'm desperate for cash and the thought of sucking your dick makes me wanna vomit.

JOHN: Perfect...you're in, right.

CLAY: What?

JOHN: I don't have to worry...cuz you're in.

Clay doesn't get it.

JOHN: You understand that you can never speak my name to anyone.

CLAY: Um. (*reminding John*) I don't know who you are.

JOHN: (*correcting him*) You know who I am.

CLAY: No, I don't.

JOHN: Well, what are you, from Mars?

CLAY: OK. Fine...you look (*shrugs*)...sort of familiar.

John laughs at this change in the "script."

JOHN: Well. This should be interesting.

CLAY: Yeah, it should be. But it isn't.

Clay produces a gun, points it at John.

JOHN: What are you doing?

CLAY: You weren't just playing the other day. I think you are done with me.

JOHN: I don't like guns.

CLAY: Since when?

JOHN: Since right now. Put it down.

CLAY: If they find out you sold your stock cuz Todd said so — odds are, you're out of a gig. And...well, where does that leave me?

JOHN: What the fuck are you doing? Put the gun down and get shy.

CLAY: No. I'm sick of this shit...I'm sick of it. If you cut me out, I'll fucking kill you...I'll do it.

Pause. John regards Clay, calmly.

JOHN: Shoot me.

Pause. Clay stares, dead-eyed, at John.

CLAY: Okay...but I'm gonna wound you first — so that you'll know I'm serious about killing you.

JOHN: Let's skip the wounding part.

CLAY: You don't have a say in it!

JOHN: Am I hostage, then?

CLAY: If you say so.

Clay shakes his head, out of ideas.

CLAY: I don't know. I don't know what to do with you. My logical mind says kill him — and make up a limerick about it... but my emotional, more fucked-up mind — says don't. Cuz you might actually deserve to be here for some reason. But what? The only good you do in this world is employ me.

JOHN: You're fired.

CLAY: When you get slapped with the insider trading ticket and your buddies take away your stealing privileges for a couple of years, where does that leave me? How are you going to support me while you're rotting in jail?

Clay smiles at John.

Huh?

Pause. John eyes Clay coldly.

JOHN: For your sake, you better be packing more than that starter's pistol.

CLAY: Oh, I wouldn't need a gun to fix you, Leech. Well, obviously.

JOHN: Fine. Kill me.

John lies back on the bed.

JOHN: Just get it over with.

Pause. Clay regards John, sighs.

CLAY: You're not afraid of dying anymore...cuz you've done that.

JOHN: Can we please just stick to the story?

CLAY: You know what really happens and you don't wanna say.

JOHN: Oh, please, just shut up and kill me.

CLAY: You were dead...you were dead and life forced itself back into you...you, of all people.

Frustrated, exhausted, scared, hungover and sad, John weeps. Pause.

CLAY: What could you possibly do — in the future — to deserve a second chance? Especially considering what you've done in the past.

JOHN: I wish you would die.

CLAY: (*scoffs*) Don't you worry... this should be a big boost to your gigantic ego, Cry Baby. You cheated death.

JOHN: I passed out!

CLAY: Ah, the revisionist history begins already. Am I watching the news? You were dead... I know what dead looks like, trust me. You were a carcass — and... something — I swear from the outside... forced its way into you... are you like one of Satan's minions or... (*angry*) What the fuck, Johnny! It has to be something to you. It has to be something.

JOHN: Why?

Pause. Clay drops the gun. Gets himself a drink.

CLAY: I know you're scared. It scares you to think about — being dead. You're freaked out, as the kids say. I know I am and I had nothing to do with it.

JOHN: Well, you strangled me!

CLAY: Whatever... I think about death all the time. It runs in the family, so I think about it every day. Don't get me wrong, I'm not suicidal.

JOHN: Oh, that's a relief!

CLAY: I'm the opposite of suicidal. I refuse to die. Tell me one thing. What did you see?... Did you see anything while you were gone or...

John scoffs.

CLAY: You know, what happened?

JOHN: I went to heaven.

Pause. Clay restrains his disgust as much as he can.

CLAY: You're a blank space where there could have been a man.

Exit Clay to the other room. John watches him go, smiles.

JOHN: Where ya goin', Dutch? (*calls*) Don't go to sleep... as long as I'm up, you're up.

CLAY: (*off*) Go fuck yourself.

Blackout.

Scene Seven:

Clay paces, frustrated and bored, talking to himself. John snorts a line of cocaine off the bedside table.

CLAY: This is a really happy story... if you tell it backwards.

JOHN: Stop pacing.

CLAY: It's a white-knuckler.

JOHN: Ja hear me?

CLAY: Not for the faint of heart — (*eyes John*) — or dim of wit.

JOHN: You'll find it doesn't make time move any faster.

CLAY: (*suddenly fuming*) I know you're not quite sharp enough to qualify as a moron, Skip, but even you can understand, that being around something like you — for an extended period of time — is sickening. You poison the air. You're fucking poison.

Repeating the word "poison" while looking at John stops Clay, cold. He exhales a brief, quiet laugh, betraying his seething rage. John smiles at Clay, enjoying his discomfort.

JOHN: You're such a candy-ass. This is nothing. This is fucking nothing. They can't take me out. Others have tried... I've been kicked down into the gutter. Literally, one time.

CLAY: I don't care.

JOHN: By my cousins. They kicked the fucking shit out of me. Jealous of my rich daddy. And just... just before I passed out — I thought... I can use this. Everything is fuel... and I did use it... it made me stronger.

CLAY: How about we invite those cousins of yours over, tonight.

JOHN: They disappeared on a fishing trip about fifteen years ago. Tragically.

CLAY: Conveniently.

JOHN: Well...people come and go. I don't know what the fuss is about...there'll be other people...there's bad shit in the world, the blade is always spinning, hoping to hit the one who least expects it. So why think about it? It doesn't make you any better to wander around on the dark side...what's wrong with feeling good? What's wrong with that?...Know what I want? I just wanna come and come and come and come and come forever...and have the taste of white chocolate in my mouth until the last shot's fired...what's wrong with that?...I don't know how those fucks got the better of me — the cousins, I mean...I was popular in school...and in college. Never studied for anything. Always found a way to get the mark I needed. That was my education, boy. Made a lot of connections there I can still use today...fucked a lot of women...drunk, freshmen girls...the softness...the small mouth...the flowery smells of delicate things...the aroma — of differences...I liked how secretive they were...the way they seemed linked to each other...in some secret way... I'm telling you, starting out — eating the right pussy is as important as having the right friends. Don't kid yourself. All those bitches had a rich daddy back home — just like mine... Man, I was so ready for it all. So ready. Right from the beginning...I knew what people wanted to see in me...that was my gift.

CLAY: Fuck, you're boring. I hope somebody blows your fucking head off and then pisses on your neck stump.

Pause. John stares at Clay.

CLAY: What? *What?*

JOHN: What do you want?

CLAY: I want to get the fuck out of here and breath some air, ya creepy fuck.

JOHN: No, what do you really want?

Pause. Clay studies John. He folds his arms, thinks.

CLAY: You could tell me what you saw when you were dead.

John approaches Clay, he's a bit menacing.

JOHN: No, I mean, in the big scheme of things, what is it you want?

CLAY: I wanna spread mirth, obviously.

JOHN: You do nothing, unless I tell you to. And you want nothing. Guys like you should come in packs of ten.

CLAY: Don't quote me, Skip. You always punch the wrong word.

JOHN: I actually want to know. Besides money — what is it you want?

*Clay gets back to his default setting. He smiles broadly.
John is calm and sure of himself.*

CLAY: I want to make you smile like you did on our wedding day, fuckface.

JOHN: You don't ever really say anything about yourself. You never mention your family...friends...or school. You mentioned your father, once. Once. But then you bristled like you'd made a mistake by bringing him up. I remember. I made a mental note of that...you're a bottomless pit of words, but you never say anything. You just blah blah blah blah blah...normal people want to make something of themselves. Now, you seem to want to be a writer. Sort of like wanting to be good at folding towels or sweeping. But right now, you're a cocksucker by trade. Am I right?

CLAY: You are one hundred percent right, my friend.

JOHN: And so far, have you achieved all of your cock sucking goals?

CLAY: Let me answer that with a song.

Clay goes to the nightstand, does a line.

JOHN: No, you haven't even excelled there. You achieve nothing because you want nothing. And because you want nothing, you are nothing.

CLAY: No. I believe nothing, so I am nothing. And as nothing, I'm free and un-killable.

JOHN: All you have to do is want it. I worked like a dog to get where I am. And sacrificed most of my life for it...but I got it because I wanted it.

CLAY: I can't have what I want, Johnny.

JOHN: Anybody can have what they want if they get out and meet the right people.

Clay snorts at this, but stops his laugh.

CLAY: No. What I want isn't possible, Simp. So there's no point in dwelling on it.

JOHN: This should be good. Tell me, cocksucker — what do you want?

CLAY: You really wanna know?

JOHN: Seriously. I do.

CLAY: Okay... I wanna go to the future.

Pause. John winces at Clay.

JOHN: Well, that's just stupid.

CLAY: Nonetheless, it's what I want.

JOHN: No, it's not. You want everything I have without playing the game.

CLAY: No, Dickhead. I wanna leave this time and travel to a time in the distant future.

Clay shades his eyes with his hand and taps his forehead twice with it, punctuating the words "distant future."

JOHN: It's a good plan.

As Clay speaks, John nods steadily, closing his eyes frequently. He has heard it all before.

CLAY: I'm like that guy in *Planet of the Apes*. You know, the original, not the Marky Mark one. I'm surrounded by fucking shaved monkeys... fucking cowards. So I was always in a Get-your-paws-off-me-you-damn-dirty-ape kind of mood. That's why I didn't do so well at civilian jobs. I'm a man out of time.

JOHN: You — are a dick.

CLAY: You're projecting, Hon.

JOHN: You're afraid to say what you really want. You're a child.

CLAY: I've accepted that what I want will never happen. And that I'm stuck in the fucking Dark Ages with you, baby.

JOHN: You need to do something with your life. You're pathetic.

CLAY: I don't need any kind of diversion, John.

JOHN: You're pathetic.

CLAY: I'm not afraid of the empty space. I embrace it. I embrace the nothing. And at least I'm not like you are, bitch — all cornholier than thou and —

JOHN: Blah, blah, blah...

CLAY: Living the easiest lie. Running scared. I'm not afraid of anything.

JOHN: Yap, yap, yap, yap, yap...

Clay folds his arms.

CLAY: I just don't belong way back here, Gomer, so what I want is to go forward a bit — maybe a few hundred years.

JOHN: I think you're afraid of everything.

CLAY: But you have to think so.

JOHN: I pity you.

John lays on his side, on the bed, his back to Clay.

CLAY: You envy me.

Seeing that John isn't looking, Clay throws a fist back and makes, just for a second, like he's going to pummel him.

CLAY: If you didn't, I'd be dead by now...in the future? When the last of the clean water dries up and the air's the scariest colour it's ever been?

John moans.

CLAY: And nothing grows? And even Lynnette's campaign to save the swamps is over. The only way they'll be able to get revenge on us, will be to ruin anything that's left from our time. Like what the zombies did to all of that guy's stuff in *Omega Man*. They'll burn art and movies, mostly. Not because they don't appreciate them or value them but because it will be the only real way to retaliate for all the deformed babies and flat, empty plains. For a sun that bakes bare flesh in minutes.

JOHN: Blah, blah, blah, blah, blah.

CLAY: And the only way to have revenge will be to forget the ones from this time, who worked so fucking hard to be remembered. In richer countries, they'll clone some of us out of the better preserved corpses. They'll raise them, then publicly execute those re-made mutherfuckers from the past. So instead of living in a culture that runs entirely on ignorant fear, it'll be little gaggles of burnt left-overs who are all about revenge. Twice a year, they'll have raves in the cemeteries, dancing up and down on your grave. And I wanna be at that party, John. I wanna help erase this time and make all of the immortals mortal again. Now, fucking tell me what you saw while you were dead.

Pause. John looks over his shoulder at Clay.

JOHN: What time is it?

He sits up, checks his watch.

JOHN: I have to make a call. Go to the other room.

Clay eyes John as John goes, quickly, to his cell phone.

JOHN: Go.

Exit Clay to the other room.

John dials, waits.

JOHN: All right...just tell me.

SFX: slowed down recording of a steady intake of breath.

Blackout.

Scene Eight:

SFX: The inhalation sound gets steadily louder, becoming a thunderous roar. It stops suddenly.

Clay emerges from the other room. John is in the mirror.

JOHN: I have to get to sleep early tonight. There'll be a lot of press at the house in the morning. The room's yours for the week, if you want it.

CLAY: No matter what happens?

John scoffs.

JOHN: What could happen?

CLAY: Don't play tough for me, Johnny. You could get gutted like a rabbit tomorrow. Don't get me wrong, I'm still planning a big party — and you better be here — but this might be one of those times when we might want to be realistic.

JOHN: No party tomorrow night. Tomorrow afternoon, once we've fixed this mess, I'm calling The Agency and we're going to do it right.

Pause. Clay regards John.

CLAY: Well... I guess you know how it all turns out, then... do you?

John smiles.

JOHN: I have a pretty good idea.

Pause. Clay regards John.

CLAY: You're a free man.

JOHN: Looks like it, yeah.

CLAY: Well. I've said it before and I'll say it again — good lawyers are worth their weight in feces... Lynnette must be relieved.

John is a bit puzzled by this.

JOHN: Well, it's her stock, too, so — yeah, I'd say she's relieved.

CLAY: That's good. It would be a shame to have some little fumble like that slice you open and scoop out your innards.

Clay stretches as John checks his hair in the mirror, turning his head to see it on every angle.

CLAY: You know what kind of shame that would be, Skip? A cryin' shame, that's what kind... Well, we should get all fucked up and play Good Priest/Bad Priest 'til they throw us out of this dump.

JOHN: It's a nice thought, but —

CLAY: I was thinkin' it might delay my death by boredom.

JOHN: I don't want to look tired on camera.

John starts out.

CLAY: Hey.

John stops.

CLAY: Seriously... tell me what you saw when you died... (*first ever*) please.

John stops. He scoffs, quietly. Pause. He studies Clay for a moment.

JOHN: Okay... you know what I saw?

CLAY: What?

JOHN: *(honestly)* Nothing... no light. No colour. No shape. Nothing.

Pause. They watch each other.

JOHN: I don't know what you want... what do you want?

Silence. They don't move. John begins to get uneasy with Clay's stare.

JOHN: Hide the wine... and don't be here when the maids come.

John starts out, stops. He goes to Clay.

JOHN: Look... it's getting obvious that we've come to the end of the road. Can't have you around right now. Okay? Don't make it ugly. Just get your stuff and go... Billy will get you a plane ticket to wherever you want.

CLAY: Business class?

JOHN: Don't ever try to contact me... I like you. But if you ever talk to anyone about me — if you even speak my name to anyone... well... you understand.

Exit John.

Pause. Clay sighs, deeply, relieved to be alone. He begins to undress. He struggles to pull off a boot.

SFX: the slowed down recording of the breath inhalation.

Clay's struggle puts him on the floor. He gives up on the boot, leans forward, presses his forehead into the floor, pulls his arms into his chest and screams. Like some animal desperate to escape its body, Clay's voice pulls itself from him with startling force.

SFX: the breath becomes a roar.

Scene Nine:

Lights on the disheveled bed. Clay lounges in a pair of shorts, chewing gum. He's holding a TV remote. He has the phone in the other hand. He laughs, heartily. There is a tightly packed knapsack and a small bag at the foot of the bed.

CLAY: I think you should be up here. I got some beer and some blow... I am. I'm ready. Don't be an ass. Come on, how often do you get to hang in a place like this, ya big wuss, just —

Clay stops abruptly when John enters.

CLAY: Never mind.

Clay hangs up, stands. He's surprised, guarded.

John has drunk himself sober and is determined to alter his consciousness. He goes directly to the nightstand. He pulls the drawer open, emptying it. Clay thinks about what to do. John picks up the bag of coke and shakes its contents out on the table.

CLAY: Hey, John.

John removes a bill, rolls it up, snorts as much coke as he can. Clay watches him, silently, until John stops, sits.

CLAY: What are you doing here?... Shouldn't you be home or...

Silence. John breathes deeply, trying to slow his panicked thoughts.

CLAY: John.

Pause. John catches his breath.

JOHN: They're going to charge us on Monday.

CLAY: Yeah, it's been on the news all day...maybe you should be — home.

Pause. John regards Clay.

JOHN: Are you trying to get rid of me?

CLAY: No.

John notices Clay's luggage. Pause.

JOHN: You're all packed.

Pause. Clay looks at his belongings.

CLAY: Yeah.

JOHN: Ready to run.

CLAY: *(tries, but can't quite scoff)* What?

JOHN: That's good. That's good.

Pause. They watch each other. Still amazed, Clay begins to enjoy this turn of events. He can't help smiling.

CLAY: You won't go to jail, John...rich guys hardly ever go to jail. And even if they do, it's like a hotel with a fence around it...I'll come visit you.

JOHN: You think this is funny?

CLAY: No. No, I don't...it's just the thought of you and Lynnette in the orange jumpsuit is sort of...cute. You have to admit.

Clay smiles at John. Pause. John regards Clay, nodding.

JOHN: You're happy.

CLAY: I'm always happy, Skip. Come on, you know what I'm like — tragedy makes me giddy.

JOHN: You're happy about this.

CLAY: No, I don't take pleasure in other people's —

JOHN: Oh, fuck-off, you little bitch!

John almost weeps. Clay sighs. Pause.

CLAY: (*guilty*) Okay. Come on... you wanna play Humiliation?... No?... We could play Dominator... *Orrr*... Arresting Officer? No, I guess not that one.

John stands, breathing heavily. He can't pick a direction in which to start pacing, so he sits again.

JOHN: I thought... I thought of you... when they told me... I looked at the lawyers and Lynnette and Chris and everybody ... and I thought of you... at a moment like that... why would I think of you?

Pause. Clay shrugs, grinning.

CLAY: I don't know.

Pause. John doesn't look at Clay.

JOHN: You were here, remember?... The day Todd called to tell me to sell the stock... you heard that conversation.

CLAY: So? So did Billy. Besides, Todd's the one who fucked you.

Don't look at me.

JOHN: Why are you packed?

CLAY: Well... I kinda assumed you were done with me since you're going... through this thing. Don't get all weird, Johnny. It's awkward enough... I'm gonna go.

JOHN: You're not done 'til I say so.

Pause. Clay nods at John, smiling at the absurdity of it.

CLAY: You know what? Sure. Okay. You're the boss.

John begins to laugh, quietly.

JOHN: I keep wishing for a heart attack... a coma.

John laughs in frustration until he cries, briefly and without trying to hide it. His exhaustion becomes more apparent.

Clay produces glasses and a bottle of Scotch. He pours a drink for each of them.

JOHN: I didn't hurt anyone... it was just money... I might have done some things I shouldn't have done. Okay. Okay. Then, I'm sorry... I am.

CLAY: Here.

John downs the drink, puts his hand out for the bottle. Clay hands it to him. John pours himself another.

JOHN: When you fall, boy... they all turn on you... because you've been in... know too much and they want you dead... maybe that's why I thought of you.

CLAY: Well, either way, it's nice that you think of me. Cheers.

Pause. John eyes Clay.

JOHN: I trust Billy... but I don't trust you.

CLAY: That's what makes the Clay ride fun. I'm exciting. And you can trust that muscle-bound nutjob all you want, but I wouldn't want to be you when he finds out he's fired.

JOHN: Billy's not fired. Not ever... no matter what... I think someone talked to that bitch reporter... the one who started this shit about Todd in the first place... why did I keep thinking of you.

CLAY: Don't be so paranoid! Everybody fucking hates you... it could have been anyone who's ever heard of you.

Pause. John thinks, stares.

JOHN: You and Billy were the only ones who knew about the stock.

CLAY: I make way more money than that fucking gorilla, plus all the cash. You're a good meal ticket, John. No one can ever take that away from you.

Pause. John stares, coldly.

JOHN: How do you know how much he makes?

Clay scoffs, a little surprised by his slip.

CLAY: I just do.

He smiles, broadly.

JOHN: I'll wipe that smile off your face... all I have to do is call Billy and tell him that you're retired... you wanna get retired?

CLAY: You can't scare me, John. I'm uncontrollable.

JOHN: You're a degenerate scrap of meat.

CLAY: (*pointing upward*) Or so it would seem!... I'm gonna go.

Clay stands, picks up his pants. John removes all of his cash, throws it at Clay.

JOHN: You're working!

Pause. Clay considers the money and John.

CLAY: Harder than you'll ever know, baby.

Pause. Clay sighs, deeply. John stares at him.

JOHN: Just... tell me you didn't talk to anyone — about anything.

CLAY: You're obsessed with the past... you're a primitive. Besides, it's rude to talk politics in polite company.

Pause. John stares at Clay.

JOHN: Why do I wanna smash your face.

Pause. Clay has no reaction.

JOHN: I wanna smash your fucking face.

CLAY: Well, see — when primates feel threatened, they often get violent. It's okay, little monkey. Let it all out.

John lunges at Clay.

Music: "50 Foot Queenie" by PJ Harvey blares.

They fight on the bed. It's an awkward, schoolyard style scuffle. Limbs flail, John struggles to dominate Clay. Clay tries out several wrestling moves. Finally, Clay breaks up laughing, throws John off and stands. Clay cackles, invigorated, moving away from the bed.

The music ends.

John pulls himself into the bedding, pressing his face into the mattress.

Clay puts his hands in his shorts, cupping his balls.

CLAY: Okay. Okay. Okay, I've got one. I'll be John and you be Clay... come on, Skip. You won't have this kind of fun in millionaire jail. It'll be all playing checkers and gettin' fucked by a bunch of pencil-dicked accountants. Come on... come on, Johnny, you paid for it.

John sits up. He laughs, bitterly, at Clay.

JOHN: No matter what... no matter what happens to me, you're still a degenerate... you'll never have what I have.

CLAY: Had.

Pause. John stands, awkwardly removing his jacket.

CLAY: How about I'll be John and you be Clay.

JOHN: How about you get over here and suck my cock.

CLAY: Ya want fries with that?

JOHN: Now.

Clay chuckles at John.

CLAY: You know what, Skip? Okay.

He spits out his gum as he goes to John.

CLAY: Even though I'm supposed to have this room to myself — and even though our dance together is way over, I'm gonna be a sport and suck your dick for old time's sake. Not only that, it's on the house.

JOHN: Wait a minute.

Clay stops. John eyes him.

JOHN: Tell me that it wasn't you...not playing anything. Just say it...say you didn't talk to that reporter.

Pause. John looks for a sign, but doesn't see one. John presses his face to Clay's chest, wanting to be smaller. He puts his arms around Clay. Clay does not move.

JOHN: It wasn't you...just say it wasn't you.

Pause. Clay peels John's arms from his waist and steps back.

JOHN: Oh, fuck.

CLAY: Well, you know it was!

JOHN: You little fucking fuck! You son of a —

CLAY: Oh, come on! You knew. As soon as you read that story, you knew who told her. Any word you've said in public in the last five years, that got you anywhere, I put in your mouth. And when you saw that article, you didn't notice me in there? You didn't notice the little phrases, the little pearls, tucked away between the fistfuls of gravel? Do you know anyone else who talks like me, you fuckin' idiot?

JOHN: But I didn't do anything to you. Why would —

CLAY: You didn't see me coming the first time Billy introduced us? Of course you did. Of course you did... that's the horror of life, John — everybody gets what they want.

Pause. John is genuinely shocked, heartbroken. He sits. Calmly, Clay gets dressed. When he is done, he gathers his things.

JOHN: Why did you do this?

Clay sighs.

CLAY: Don't ruin a beautiful moment, Johnny. This is the last time we'll ever see each other, so don't be an ass, all right?... I sent a speech to your house. Don't change anything in it. You'll have Chris arrange a press conference. Lynnette should be there, too. Don't answer questions. Just say the words. You'll be all right.

JOHN: I don't understand... what's happening.

Clay goes to John, takes John's face in his hands. It's neither menacing nor tender.

CLAY: You know why I'm here. You know who I am... you at least have an inkling.

JOHN: You never said anything about your past. Never once mentioned anything that was in your file. There was a background check.

CLAY: I wrote that file, John. Listen — I have a new project starting up and I have to learn a new accent, so —

JOHN: Who's paying you?

Clay laughs, snorting a little.

JOHN: Who's paying you to do this to me?

CLAY: It's not a paying gig, Johnny.

JOHN: What the fuck! What the fuck are you doing?

CLAY: Don't make it worse. Please.

JOHN: You're dead. As soon as you leave this room, you're fucking dead!

CLAY: No.

JOHN: You don't think so, you little piece of shit?

CLAY: No. I have insurance.

JOHN: I swear to god —

CLAY: Look, John. We have video of you going down on me in the car outside Le Bistro. 'Member? Lynnette's birthday? You said you wanted something to kill the taste of the Steak Tartar.

Pause. John is amazed, finally beginning to understand.

JOHN: (*quietly*) Who's "we"?

CLAY: If anything happens to me, that troubling bit of historical porn gets posted on the net tomorrow. And trust me — you don't want that. I had them blur my face and even I'm not all that comfortable with it.

JOHN: Why... why would you do that?

CLAY: Cuz see, the believers don't have a problem with you being a liar and a thief and a fraud, John — but this... this is sex. Scary, dirty sex a long way out of wedlock. And I think we all know those redneck dog-fuckers will have a big problem with that. So, it's my insurance.

JOHN: (*smiling*) No, no, no, no, no. This is a game! This is all — it's a new game you're starting.

CLAY: Think about that for a minute, John. I'm not playing.

JOHN: What do you want from me?

CLAY: Seventy-five dollars and your Ted Nugent records. Nothing! What the fuck could you have that I'd want?

JOHN: Then why? Why?

CLAY: Because... look — what goes around comes around on account of we make it come around.

JOHN: Who's "we"?

CLAY: I don't know. I don't know any of their names — but I know how many of us there are. And trust me — stepping on you and a few CEOs is just a little test drive. We're everywhere, John. We're fucking everywhere, now... you old school bitches might write the news, but we don't need popular opinion on side. We don't need anyone.

JOHN: I've always been good to you. Hired you right out of school. No experience.

CLAY: Johnny. Wake up! There's a war on... and we intend to win it. One asshole at a time.

John dials on his cell phone.

CLAY: Billy won't answer that call, Skip. He's my ride to the airport. ... Don't send anyone to look for us. And don't change the speech. Just say the words.

Exit Clay.

Scene Ten:

SFX: a slowed down inhalation of breath reaches a certain point and then continues without building or ending.

Golden morning lights rise.

John is suddenly sober. Seemingly aware of the audience, he cleans himself up as best he can. His hands shake a little. He moves downstage, steps into light. There are intermittent camera flashes.

JOHN: Lynnette...couldn't be here. She um...she sends her regrets...just let me say this, please...I won't be taking questions. This is all I have to say... "I know that I have disappointed my family and friends. I know that what I did is inexcusable...but I also know in my heart...that God will forgive me...no matter how we may stray from the path, he will lead us home...that is my firm belief...now...I know I don't deserve it, but I am asking the people...for their forgiveness... (*fighting tears*) because I can handle whatever the judge gives me...whatever the press and the mudslingers can throw my way...I can take it...but I can't live with the shame of knowing that I have disappointed the people who gave me my career in politics...I want all of you to know that I am deeply sorry...and it is my sincere hope that, someday, you will forgive me"... That's all I have.

Exit John in a flurry of flashes.

SFX: Traffic.

The lights cross-fade to a downstage wash.

Scene Eleven:

Enter Clay, pushing a baby carriage. There is white netting net over it. He wears the sort of suit that a trendy academic type would wear. Sunglasses, a baby bag over his shoulder.

John enters, from the opposite side. He wears a bad trench coat, sunglasses, holds a briefcase.

They meet downstage. Clay smiles at John. John shakes his head.

JOHN: Well. Look at you.

CLAY: John. Wow...look at you.

JOHN: Don't tell me...have you given up the war for family life?

CLAY: Naw. No retreat, no surrender, mutherfucker. You look good, John.

JOHN: Thank you. I feel good. I'm selling insurance now.

They laugh.

JOHN: Can you believe that shit?

CLAY: Everybody needs insurance.

JOHN: That's what I tell them.

CLAY: You ever see any of the old gang?

JOHN: No.

CLAY: And Lynnette, she's...

JOHN: She — um — she's not doing so well.

Clay nods.

CLAY: I'm sorry to hear that.

JOHN: (*shakes an image of her*) Lynn...hears voices now, she says.

John laughs, quietly.

JOHN: Well. Everything rots. Have to grab whatever you can before it's over.

CLAY: I suppose so.

JOHN: You ever see Billy?

CLAY: Sure.

JOHN: And he's...

CLAY: He's Billy. He's cutting himself for the shock value, lately. We don't encourage him, we don't discourage him...listen... I wasn't completely honest with you when we saw each other last time —

JOHN: What? Really?

CLAY: Seriously. It's always bothered me that I didn't tell you the whole truth about something.

John removes his sunglasses, nods. Pause.

JOHN: I see. There is no tape of me blowing anybody, is there?

CLAY: No.

JOHN: I knew it.

CLAY: I mean, it's not that. The blow job video is safe. Don't worry about it.

JOHN: So... (*scoffs, whispers*) Fuck... what did you lie about?

CLAY: Here's the thing — I did what I did to you because I believe in all that Fight The Powers That Be and Stick It To The Man type shit, but it was a little personal, too.

JOHN: A little.

CLAY: I know you won't remember this — but when I was fourteen, my science class did a presentation in your office about the water table around our neighbourhood. How it was being poisoned by the pesticide plant. We explained how all of the chemicals seeping into the soil were extremely dangerous and you said you were going to help us out. But then three weeks later, you signed off on that bogus environmental report that said the water was harmless — like it was just colourful or something. You said people needed more education on the topic, but I didn't need any more fucking education.

JOHN: What are you talking —

CLAY: My dad, my grandmother and my brother, my little brother — John... they all died of cancer within three years of each other... we lived a quarter of a mile from that plant... my mother used to tell us to hold our breath when we went by on the way to school.

JOHN: Look, I don't even remember the —

CLAY: I've buried so many of them, my next embalming is free.

Even though it's likely to be my own, a good deal is a good deal.

JOHN: I'm sorry, I just don't see —

CLAY: Yeah, yeah, yeah... the past wants me, John... and sooner or later, the past gets everything.

JOHN: This is insane. That had nothing to do with —

CLAY: Lynnette's family owns the insecticide company that made that mess, John. And who bought the report that said those chemicals were harmless?

JOHN: I don't think —

CLAY: You, bitch. You did.

Clay removes his shades.

CLAY: After the last funeral, I promised myself, that I'd expose you to the light.

JOHN: This is absolutely —

CLAY: When I joined up with these losers I'm with now, they had a list of sixty dinosaurs to make extinct within ten years. I picked you because you had the chance to clean up that plant and you chose not to.

Pause. John shakes his head, dumbfounded.

JOHN: Well... I don't know what to say. I'm at a loss for words.

CLAY: I fucking hate words. I am not a writer, you know. But I got myself hired by you... because our evolution depends on your extinction... I believe in evolution, John. That's the fundamental difference between us. I accept reality — and you're a cunt.

JOHN: You used to pride yourself on not having any beliefs... you used to be clean. Now you'll pass it all down to...

John looks in at the baby. Pause.

JOHN That's... that's not a baby.

CLAY: No.

Pause. John looks at Clay, at the inside of the carriage, at Clay.

JOHN: That's... what is it?

CLAY: It's half of a mutant pig fetus.

Pause. John looks at Clay, at the inside of the carriage, at Clay.

JOHN: What is it?

CLAY: It's exactly one half of a mutant pig fetus. It's for a surprise photo-op that's going to follow the revelation that much of the other half of this little freak was fed to several visiting Royals, this morning. Mutant pig fetus is part of a complete breakfast.

John laughs.

JOHN: That's... why? What's the point of that?

CLAY: Just to prove that we can get to anyone... and to say that maybe pig feed shouldn't be made of pigs... and we're having a bit of fun with an idiot monarchy. Fucking inbred chimps. Every day is Halloween for those assholes.

JOHN: Well...you'll go to jail for this.

CLAY: I won't get caught. I'm just leaving the carriage outside their embassy with a note, so...how was it?

JOHN: What?

CLAY: Millionaire jail.

JOHN: It wasn't that bad...I thought of you, now and again...I got fucked with a lot until I beat the shit out of this Haliburton prick with a heart problem...then it was sort of like being in school again. I met a lot of people. It's actually a good place to network, because no one can get away from you ...plus prison sex has this — romance about it...a meaning, even...so...wasn't all bad. (*smiles*) There's no reason for any of this, you know.

CLAY: I know.

Pause. John grins at someone in his head.

JOHN: We just fill in the blanks as we go.

CLAY: Most of us have them filled in for us. That's a trip, but the sweet part is that the blanks don't really exist.

JOHN: And the blanks don't even exist.

CLAY: Reality exists, though.

JOHN: Yeah.

CLAY: But nothing else.

JOHN: Nothing else.

CLAY: No blanks to fill in, anywhere.

John looks at Clay, laughs heartily.

JOHN: No... but it's hard to resist.

Pause. Clay smiles at John.

CLAY: Nothing changes. Or if it does, it doesn't change quickly enough for me to notice. I'm a predator, right? Made for seeing things that are moving.

JOHN: That's how it is sometimes.

CLAY: I can stare into the chaos — and lose myself. It's a relief.

John nods.

JOHN: Yeah, yeah... and you're still in the war.

CLAY: I know. Man... belief is crack.

John nods.

CLAY: I know it's pointless to fight. I just don't know what to do with my hands if there's no scuffle going on.

JOHN: I don't fight. I had to surrender because I'm in a drug rehabilitation program. I didn't like that one bit. I was already down a peg — or ten. So I didn't need to hear about surrendering.

CLAY: Rehab for what?

JOHN: Oh, come on, you know. I was always high — or drunk.

CLAY: But... drugs are all you have.

JOHN: No, there's more to life than getting —

CLAY: Not for you. Not for you, Johnny. You need some kind of relief from...well, from — you know — bein' you.

JOHN: I'm grateful for my sobriety.

CLAY: Then they suckered you good...well. I guess we reap what we sow.

JOHN: Yeah.

CLAY: So what?

Delighted, they laugh. Pause.

JOHN: Well...well. (*to the tune of "I'll See You Around"*) I hope you die.

CLAY: I will.

John passes him. Clay starts off. He stops.

CLAY: Hey.

John stops.

JOHN: Yeah.

Pause. Clay considers John for a moment.

CLAY: I love you.

JOHN: I know.

Pause. John considers the inevitability of it.

JOHN: I know... I love you, too.

CLAY: (*nods*) Yeah.

They consider each other for a moment.

SFX: the traffic noise increases.

Exit John stage left, exit Clay stage right.

THE END.

GEMINI

GEMINI

The house lights fade as deeply ominous, rhythmic music plays. Spotty white lights rise.

There is a comfortable armchair, centre. There is an old-fashioned backdrop: Fields and distant, mist-covered mountains. The paint is faded, the canvas is worn and the pastoral scene is hanging crookedly.

Two women enter. They dance and toss rose petals in their path. Both are dressed in black, sleek, paramilitary uniforms. Over these, they wear tutus made from shredded hospital bed sheets. One has a bottle of wine. They're a little drunk, a little high. When they have covered most of the downstage area, the first dancing goon begins to stare, blank-faced at the audience. The second, looks out, opens her mouth as wide as she can, screws up her face, sticks out her tongue with a silent BLAH. The first begins to dance again, but it is little more than a few hops and gestures. She looks off right. Pause. The second dancing goon, throws her near empty basket of petals upstage and walks off. The first looks out again, sneers a little, makes her exit. Just as she enters the wings, she has a violent confrontation with someone we can hardly see.

Joe enters from the opposite side. The second goon enters, exits when she sees Joe. He is about twenty-nine. He wears an ill-fitted black suit, black shoes. He hasn't shaved for a few days. He's feeling seedy. His left hand is wrapped in a strip of bloody gauze. Joe looks up at the back of the house. He yells.

JOE: Will you turn that fucking music off!

He cannot be heard. He yells once more.

JOE: Will you turn that—

The music stops suddenly.

JOE: —fucking music off!

Joe sits. He fumbles with a bottle of brandy, sloppily fills a snifter. He then puts a cigarette in his mouth, realizes that he doesn't have his lighter and tosses the cigarette.

JOE: I want to thank you for indulging me and for... I know this is unorthodox so I just want to say that I applaud your... imagination... I think that if you hear me out, you'll have to agree that I'm... street-friendly and... all right.

He clears his throat.

JOE: Who knows where all of this is going, people in movies and television shows say.

He laughs.

JOE: Sorry. All right, then. Okay. Let's see... some *prrrrrrick* next door got himself a motorcycle. He goes out there and he revs that piece of shit thing for half of the morning and most of the night. Back and forth. Always on the go. "Are we out of envelopes? Well, hey! I've got my motorcycle right outside. I'll be right back!" Now... if this were a movie, you know what would happen next. I'd say, "Hey, buddy! Shove that fuckin' motorcycle straight up your ass!" Then he'd say something and then I'd say something and so on. Back and forth, until there's an event. Crowbar to the head or something. Let's hide the body. Then at the end of the first act, say — oh, around page thirty, I'm in jeopardy and that calls for me to do something extremely difficult. Why, it seems impossible. That calls for — more action... my neighbour and I say things to show the audience our one or two characteristics, while running and jumping. When you're a tap dancer with no talent, you just dance fast and move your arms a lot. Then at the end of act two comes (*a peculiar, metallic voice finishes the line with him*) — the moment of decision. "Should I tell the pigs where I hid the body? Will I run out on Tasha? Hey! I was set up. Framed or something by James Woods." Or whatever. So. Misadventures that move the remarkable story forward, make for an act two, which culminates in the explosive meeting of the good guy and the bad guy and the tied up girl. Some suspense, a few explosions. Then the hero — me — who has been forced to take action and make the impossible choice, has thusly grown and stares steel-eyed over some perfect resolve: "I'll tell ya one thing, Tasha, what I don't want for Christmas...is another motorcycle. Let's go home." "Is it really over, Brad?" "Yeah, baby. It's over. It's all over." They kiss and walk away. Some shitty radio song plays. If this were a movie, we'd know what to expect from each other...but this is probably as real as it's ever going to get.

Sound: Glass smashing off stage, some incoherent yelling.

JOE: Anyway...my cousin Philip used to have this philosophy so I killed him. I said let's go fishing. So we did. But then I had to overpower him which wasn't easy — and hold his head under water to kill him. It's called drowning when you do that. I drownded him — big time. Anyway, like I said — he had this philosophy so...you know, it's that old thing if you could go back in time and kill Adolf Hitler, would you do it? I wouldn't. I'd go further back in time and fix his father's father's brakes. I'm the only one who thinks ahead. Remember that. My cousin Phil's entire family is insane. Fucked all the way up. And because of them, Philip had this philosophy, this belief system, so...I mean, of course everyone's entitled to their opinion — but when they start telling it to people — and he was trying to tell me, for years — convince me, maybe...I didn't enjoy doing it. I was enjoying fishing. I like catching fish. That part was great. We don't even eat them. Just let them go with a warning. You know, when you have to hold your cousin's head under water and his eyes are bulging, looking up at you and he can't believe it and you can't even tell him why you're doing it...and he kicks ya right in the nuts and there's all that splashing...it's a trip. I couldn't say, Listen, sorry, man, but I have to kill you because you have this belief system and I have to protect the world from you...there've been a few occasions when I have felt extremely guilty about that...but at the same time, I know I did something good for all of humanity, so...and nobody can prove anything...so technically, it didn't even happen. He gets upgraded to Missing. You know how that goes...why are you doing this? ...You know what I want. It's not much, believe me... (*amazed*) No?...all right, then...let us continue.

Pause.

JOE: If I could fly under space and be in several places at once, I'd have to hunt myself down and drown me in a river. See, I've developed this belief system and...I'm kidding. I'm just tryin' to scare ya. I'm not insane. I don't believe anything.

Sound: A dramatic symphony — frantic strings.

JOE: Here are ten stories. Or at least, what I believe to be stories ...and what I believe to be ten. Not poems. Not speeches.

The music ends with a flourish.

JOE: Ten Stories!

A 6os psychedelic wash envelopes him and the words "Number One" are projected on the floor. Sound: An old mono recording by a bad violin player.

JOE: Number One: You come home late on Friday, curl on your fucking futon and dream of a world without analysis.

The psychedelic wash goes out, the words "Number One" disappear as a faint, green triangular light grows. Joe steps into it. The words "Number Two" are projected below it.

Sound out.

JOE: Number Two: How long have you been standing there, pretending that you might make a move?... How long have you been waiting there like that? Hoping that no one sees just how weak...how weak you are...whether you know it or not, you're waiting for me...and waiting for me to come along must be like a long terrible marriage...

Green light out.

The centre area is suddenly lit with layers of leaves. The words "Sympathy Vote" are projected below.

JOE: Number Three: I miss you for when we would sit on your roof and scream at your neighbours. I miss you for when we did acid and went to bingo. I miss you for long, dead-lawn Saturdays. For the tricks you could do with a penny, for your breath on my arm and for sleep.

The original lighting returns. Joe takes a drink after every line of the following:

JOE: Number Four: I don't hold my breath when I go swimming. I won't hold anyone's hand when I go for a walk. I don't talk to strangers. I don't eat candy. I don't hold my breath when I'm under water...I don't take notice of any splash, but my own. I won't come when you call. I won't be what you wished for. I won't be concerned. I will not be distracted.

Blackout. New washes of light rise: red, gold, and yellow. The words "Son of Overlord" are projected on the floor in 1950s movie poster script.

Sound: Frantic symphony strings, the sort for high action.

JOE: Number Five...

Playing both parts, expertly, Joe re-enacts his favourite scene from his all-time favourite movie, Son of Overlord. *(This movie does not actually exist.)*

OVERLORD: Do you fear me now, Doctor? I will crush you with my awesome power!

DOCTOR L: *(ala Basil Rathbone)* I was a fool to try to play God! You — you will become still more powerful, more cruel. If there is not even a shred of humanity left in this, your mutated form — then God help us all! God help us all, Richard!

OVERLORD: Do not call me Richard! I was your assistant once, but now, thanks to your improbable experiment, I am Overlord! I now posses the knowledge of fifty millennia! You are mere vermin to me!

Dr. L turns away for his dramatic speech.

DOCTOR L: "Turning and turning in a widening gyre — The fal—"

Joe mimes being strangled by Overlord's powerful, mammoth grip.

OVERLORD: *(While strangling Doctor L)*: You are dainty, Doctor L. Small and puny! You would not make even a decent foot soldier in my Legion of Doom. Therefore, YOU MUST BE DESTROYED!

Sound: The music swells and stops suddenly as Overlord pulls Dr. L's head off.

The lighting for story Number One returns. The words "Number Nine" are projected on the floor.

JOE: Number Six: You rise from your fucking futon on Saturday morning. Go barefoot across a cool patch of magazines, pass the mirror and don't look, to the bathroom, foul mouthed and full of evil deeds. Pee, coffee, water, uniform, more coffee. Then it's marching to Job. At Job, there is only to do and you won't be distracted.

The original lights return. The word "Eleven" is projected on the floor.

JOE: Number Seven: I'm making this up as I go. It's not about anything, but I've come to believe that there are (*partially to someone off stage*) ELEVEN MYSTERIES OF THE UNIVERSE!

Sound: A weird, discordant musical sting.

JOE: The first is that everyone sees everything and pretends not to. That's mysterious. That is the first mystery of the universe. The second is Ancient Prophesies! Ancestor caca. Even if a bunch of those Ancient Prophecies turn out to be true, who gives a shit? By the time you know, you're dead. The third mystery of the universe is math. The sixth is that the universe is universally mysterious, like dark glasses, but there are two rules that apply to everything in it. A: No matter what you take off of it, its always under something. And B: "To be or not to be" is not an example of a literal question. There is only to be. So get used to it. The fourth of the eleven mysteries is that there is no such thing as the good, the bad, or the ugly. The fifth of the eleven mysteries of this and — I think — all universes in the surrounding area, is that there is no such thing as nothing. Numbers begin at one, not zero.

Momentarily fed up, he sighs, shakes his head at us.

JOE: There's always something, isn't there? The tenth of the eleven is that every judgment is only a refusal to perceive. The eleventh mystery of the universe is the illusion of variation. I've come to accept all of this because it explains me... it shows that, you know... you have absolutely nothing to fear. (*as Overlord*) I show you my armour and my belly! But of course, I have the proof, too. I can back up everything I say. I talk the walk, baby. There's numbers for everything.

A large, horizontal, rectangular light replaces the original light.

JOE: Number Eight: Seven months ago, I was in a hotel, marching across the lobby, and this woman stops me and says, very casually, as though we knew each other, "The sky always doesn't fall." I said, "Excuse me." She kept walking. I followed her. She shook me in under a minute. I knew then that I shouldn't have smoked those last five hundred thousand cigarettes. *The sky always doesn't fall.* I took this to mean, "Start working without a net." So I did... that was great advice and it was free. Ya hear me? Free!

Sound: Bright 70s game show Muzak plays.

JOE: Number Nine: My father's a homosexual, but he lived as a heterosexual so that everybody would like him. It didn't work. Nobody really likes him except me and my sisters and my mother and my mother's slam, Gordon. She has this guy — her slam, she calls him — Gordon and he lives in their basement. He owns a bike shop downtown, but all he ever does is watch TV and read newspapers like a simp. He's the reason I'm in so much shit, really. Boy, I shouldn't be saying any of this, because if you say something long enough, you start to believe it and then your cousin has to take you to a river and drown you until you know better. Besides — you know the gag order... get it? Cuz you're all gagged.

He laughs a big fake laugh, stops and steps into a box of

blue light. Sound: a short bit of a 1920s recording of a lonely harmonica. It plays on a loop. Lights: a wheat field at dusk. Joe talks like a movie drill sergeant.

JOE: Why don't you shut your mouth and listen... listen! This is serious business here. What do you think you're doing?... Are you on something? Are ya drunk?... Well, then what's your problem? You look all twisted... you sound like a fucking idiot... this is serious shit you're into now... and I brought you out here, to show you the sky, you know, the stars — I'm trying to make a point. I'm trying to — shut-the-fuck-up!... I'm trying to make a point — I'll tell you... look up.

A star field forms over the theatre.

JOE: Look at the stars. LOOK UP at the stars!... Now, just look... do you see?... Good. Are you looking at the stars? Good, now ...you...have NOTHING TO SAY!!!... STOP TALKING!!!

The lights snap back, but to a variation of the way they were. Sound out.

JOE: There's your ten stories.

Sound: a tiny band plays a brash TA-DAH!

He bows.

JOE: Some of you may feel that most, or even all of them were not stories at all. Some of you may feel that they were raw and adventurous. Nay, pieces of light in a sea of gloom. So, I'm in the confessional on the Vatican website, right? And I'm writing my confession, getting it all off my chest and its going great, but then it occurs to me — how do I know this site isn't run by the secret police? How do I know they're not making subtle changes in my brain's electromagnetic field? How do I know they're not watching me do this? Well, I don't know.

And then it occurs to me — what difference does it make if they are? So I confess, so what? Something's got to happen, right? Then a few days later, I get arrested for assault.

He stands still, facing straight ahead for half a second as a camera flashes.

JOE: That's not even worth going into. Suffice it to say I beat the shit out of a clown at the mall. Anyway, I know they want me for more than that. I know and they know. The detective keeps casually quoting from my confession on the net and I pretend not to notice. They know I canceled Philip, but they can't prove it because they can't find the body and they never will. They're up to zero on the evidence meter. But they figure they can intimidate me and cajole me and smack me around and bore the fuck out of me, but I won't give it up. The only reason I beat up the clown was because Gordon — my mother's slam — pissed me off... in a way that I can't even tell you. I go, "Lend me a hundred dollars" and he goes, "No." So I'm just seething, walking through the mall, on my way to bewilder those little pricks at Radio Shack and I see this clown. There's this happy, smiley face clown, dancing through the mall saying hello hello hello hello and he's handing out flyers. He shoves one of his bright yellow flyers in my face and it's an ad for Gordon's bike shop and I just fuckin' lose it. I'm kicking the shit out of this clown and people are screaming and yelling like it's the end of the fuckin' world. These assholes from The Gap are hauling me off of him going, "Are you insane? Are you out of your mind?" And I'm goin' "He's a clown!" Anyway ...the pigs are grilling me, telling me about all of the bad things that are going to happen to me. They pretend to have this notion that there's a punishment for every crime, that we reap what we sow. And I'm thinking, Since when? In movies, sure. James Woods gets shot by the hit man who isn't quite dead and falls in the pool and the lead actor who got shot but not enough to scar him too badly unties the girl and saves her. That's the magic of Hollywood... When I become a moderate fascist dictator, what the hell am I supposed to do with the police? What the hell am I supposed to do with James Woods? And what do you care? Well...some of you care...and some of you wish I would just shut the fuck up or do some jokes. Very well. This is still a democracy. So. Mob rules. (*aside*) Fucksake. Here are ten funny jokes for you...at least, these are what I believe to be jokes and what I believe to be funny. Here we go. Ten jokes. Let's see. Oh, this good.

Sound: Soft and slow lounge lizard piano.

JOE: Until recently, I've never been in trouble with the law. I got some grief in a restaurant last winter, that's about it. I was asked to leave because I kept singing and singing and I don't really have a very good singing voice. They threw me out. So I went back to settle up. I walked backwards to the restaurant where I was inspired to sing and that was a really hard thing to do on a beautiful Sunday morning in May when the birds were growling and the police were laughing and the children were barking and the grass was creeping. I walked backwards to prove a point. I returned my diner's card and I said to the demon in charge, "I want to shoot you"...I couldn't pull the trigger, though. Some kind of moral question kept nagging at me. Killing the person who manages the restaurant, rather than the person who owns it, seemed inappropriate. But then, following that logic, there's something wrong with murder, too. And if murder's wrong, what the fuck are we supposed to do when somebody won't let go of the distant past and they become the gum in the gears of the great machine that is about to create a truly glorious empire?

Sound out. He smiles.

JOE: That was funny. Here's another joke.

Bad, presentational TV acting.

JOE: Two white guys are sitting around the local garage one morning, getting their cars fixed. And one white guy says to the other white guy, "You know, Steve, sometimes I wonder what it's all about. What does it all mean? One day just seems to blur into the next." And the other white guy says, "Cheer up, Bill. You're not Bad Luck Louie." "Who's Bad Luck Louie?" Bill inquires. And the other white guy says, "Well, I'll tell ya. Bad Luck Louie was a hero of mine. Why, when I was a boy, Louie — or Good Luck Louie, as he was known then — was the first baseman for our hometown softball team. He was a local legend. Everybody loved Good Luck Louie." "Well, I hate to interrupt you, Steve," the other white guy says, "because I really am enjoying this yarn, but tell me, how did Good Luck Louie become Bad Luck Louie?" And the other one says, "Someone beat him to death with his lucky bat 'cause he talked like this." All right, here's a better one. A Priest, a Rabbi and a Stripper are at sea, in a row boat. They're not stranded or anything, they're just going for a boat ride. And the priest seems to have this little epiphany and says, "The fearless will carry wings in their pockets; clipped and dried for a good scent and a fast getaway." So the Rabbi and the Stripper peel off their human masks, reveal their alien monster heads and eat him. That's how that one ends. That was funny. Here's another one. How many armies does it take to unscrew a light bulb? Actually, I'd like to withdraw that last remark, Doctors. Although it wasn't meant to be, it could have been interpreted as political. And you know how passionate politics can get. And see, I don't really have any politics of my own, I just go along with what everybody else says...

Gunshot. Another. A body hits the floor off-stage.

JOE: I don't think about politics or law or whether or not the dinosaurs were warm- or cold-blooded. When I hear the word politics, no matter what the context, I think of Cults in America. I think of money. Napoleon. Pol Pot. I think of Margaret Thatcher limping to the bathroom with a woody.

Sad old men blowing Satan. I think, of course, of the CHURCH. Men — wearing white, coz you know how pure men are. I think of the oily, Victorian residue that still permeates huge baggy pockets of the whole rotten stinking world. The spin doctors, and the tired old, sad old ass-lickers. And the tired old, sad old believers. When I hear the word politics, I think about money, then I think of mites. If I continue from this point, however, with "Hmmmm...politics," I will be in REM sleep within seconds. This is my gift. You see, like you, I've seen enough pasty old carrion in business suits, telling some poor fucker somewhere what he or she should think about things that the poor fucker will never really know anything about. Been to school, thanks. And I've seen the news. You need a good suit to rule the world. That's pretty much the whole story. "Wow! He's really full of outrage now," you might think. Or "That's tellin' 'em! There'll be a revolution and the world will be taken back from the pigs of the world and — The world! The world! And oh, my God, The Whole World!" It's just not that big. And before you decide my fate — if not the fate of The World — I want to give each of you the opportunity to visit the sign-up sheets outside. If you'd like to join me now, that would be great because I am going to rule the world and crush my enemies with an iron fist. Just — not right now. Right now, I'm having fun being here with all of you. Yeah! See? It's infectious!

Like an actor turned infomercial pitch-man:

JOE: Here's my plan for when I become a moderate fascist dictator. A: Seek out the most passionate and sure, from both the left and the right. Make certain that their views are clear — and their hearts are strong. B: Put them in an enormous room and let them talk and talk and talk and talk and talk at each other until their fucking eyes bleed. Who gives a shit? The rest of us will be at the beach. When I become a moderate fascist dictator — everybody goes to the beach. I'll explain when the time comes. You'll like it, I swear...because I love you... I love everything about you... and I respect you... and I will never let you down. But never mind that. Here's some dirt for you. Everybody likes dirt. My parents have decided that they want all legal ties between us broken — like a divorce. They can do this to their own blood because they have no imagination. The unclean spirit had just been snatched from them and sat... mortified... in the custody of the slavering constabulary, while they were on the phone goin'— "Yeah, Marvin, how do we get out of this deal?" So — so, you can imagine... my heavy heart...

He almost cries, then recovers, instantly.

JOE: ...I have this hold on them, though. I'm very charismatic. Especially to... intelligent people, like you... I hope you realize that I'm sincere... I'm not just saying words. I'm not like my lawyer. My lawyer sticks to the furniture. He had me tell him about how I didn't kill Philip or even bury him where no one can find him. He already knew, of course, but he wanted to hear how true it could sound. Over and over... he's easy to scare and that's been my only form of entertainment since we ran out of movies. And you know, a few weeks ago, you were right. I needed my rest. I'm glad to have been here... but the big day is coming... and I would like to begin it with a clean slate... look at my face. Jesus, I'm cute. I'm like a puppy. Especially when I look at you with that little smirk that says, "What do you say you sit here and breathe through a wet rag while you listen to me rant for four and a half hours?"

Sound: A helicopter. Joe produces a handgun. Red lights flash. He points it upward.

JOE: "You framed me Bubba and you better let Tasha go, or I'll detonate the whole shitload now and we're all fucked!"

Sound out.

JOE: "Should I tell the pigs where I hid the body? Will I run out on Tasha? Hey! I was set up. Framed or something." Try to imagine that! You can't. It's unimaginable. Movie magic. The stuff dreams are horked out of.

He drops the gun, gets a drink.

Sound: a mangled tape of the "Eleven Mysteries" and the "Joke" section plays. We hear the audience in it. Under this — Sound: Actual disasters, trauma, scraps of bad transistor radio music. Sound out.

JOE: Like most clever children, I can get into absolutely any computer anywhere, right? And you know where all the big secrets are going? Not to the sad, old, tired, old geriatric clown show we call the government. No, all of the most valuable information goes to the world's Ten Richest People. There are six of them. I've written their names in blue ink, somewhere on the wall in that corridor. Anyway, the point is, according to my source at Dreamland it's impossible for people to fly under space and to other planets. It can't be done.

Sound: the frustrated scream of someone at the back of the house.

JOE: SHUT-UP! You shut the fuck up! We sat through your tired old song that made absolutely no fucking sense, so shut your hole!

He is perfectly still for a moment, measuring his rage. Silence. He regains his composure.

JOE: You know, a lot of kind folks have given me a lot of good advice over the years. And when I become a moderate fascist dictator... they're all fucked... I've collected a lot of expensive information... I have everything required to — literally — take over the entire world. Every square metre of it... wait 'til you see the uniforms. You're gonna piss yourself. Everybody gets really big shoes. Of course, the uniform is optional — I'm not an animal. Did you ever have that dream where you're part human and part seagull and you're on a platform waiting for a train and it's raining? You start to shiver and you shake so much that bits of you start to fall off. And at first it's just the bird bits so you're not all that concerned. But then you realize that your whole body is falling apart and then you wake up and realize that it's not a dream... you ever have that one?... Well, no. Nobody has. (*eyeing the audience*) Tonight, maybe... I sweep up after the dance. You fuckers go to the hall and have the time of your life, dancing up and down. Then I have to go in at eight o'clock in the shitty morning and clean up. Mop up the dust and ashes and piss drops and puke... lots of cool stuff comes out of people! That was a funny joke. Let's play a game. I'll be a corpse and you try to guess who I was.

He lies on the floor, twisted.

JOE: Okay. Who was I?... Come on, look at my hands... FUCK YOU PEOPLE ARE STUPID! I'm that guy... from that movie! Never mind. I have some more jokes and they're really, really funny. God, I love a good joke like when some clown comes up to me and tells me a joke. I love that. Here's a good joke...

Silence. Joe seems suddenly tired. He takes a few breaths.

JOE: I'm sorry. Forget everything I've said up to this point... I have exactly one half ounce of brain... and it's on manic. I'm sorry. Fuck me... I've got a brain like a hungry pigeon... roving in a field of soggy popcorn... my parents didn't believe in contraception. They were like mad scientists. I'm not supposed to talk about them, even to friends like you, because of the gag order. Maybe at some point in the future, though. My cousin Philip used to talk a lot about the future. Now he's dead and that's great. I'm a Gemini. I don't believe in much of anything, but astrology makes sense to me. Because if the universe has, as many physicists and astrologers believe, a unified structure — if it is one, coherent entity — all movements within it, such as the movements of celestial bodies and the movements of people through the world, are unified ...right? Sure. Everything in the universe is composed of atoms, and these minute systems display a kind of "intelligence" on the dreamy quantum level. Within every atom, infinitesimally small ideas of things exist and cease to exist in moments so infinitesimally short that time does not apply to them. Infinitesimally. Infinitesimally. Astrology, the map of our lives, is our only hope in achieving enlightenment. And even if it's all garbage, who gives a shit? It only takes a second to read. Further to this, all of the four known forces of the universe are acting upon everything, always. We are everything and everything is us, goddamn it. It's a trap!

Four 1950s style abstract cut-outs descend.

JOE: The strong nuclear force, the weak nuclear force, electromagnetism and gravity. The fifth force of the universe is, as yet, unknown.

A pathetic question mark dangles alongside "gravity."

JOE: Some people think it's folk music.

A cut-out of an acoustic guitar descends.

JOE: It's not, though.

The guitar disappears.

JOE: Slight electromagnetic fluctuations in the Earth have a profound effect on our ability to comprehend what's happening around us. This is why dogs get hyper before earthquakes and people say ridiculous things. The shifting of the planet's plates, the grinding, produces a kind of electromagnetic fart.

Changes in the electromagnetic field distort the dog's ability to perceive its surroundings and it makes us see apparitions, lights. Angels. Profound emotions well up in people who have been subject to electromagnetic twisters, but usually, electromagnetism is our friend. Gravity, of course, holds the amazingly repetitive forms of the universe intact and keeps us from flying off the ball. It acts on all matter equally, but not all matter is equal. Small mass, small gravity. Big mass, Easter Sunday.

He laughs his big, fake laugh, shakes his head and sighs.

JOE: I'm a scamp! The strong nuclear force keeps atomic bits in their controlled chaos. And for us, prevents the embarrassment of melting. The weak nuclear force is what caused the Enterprise to crash on that planet where green women are compelled to dance, badly, for Canadian hams in press board girdles. The universe and everything in it is only made of one thing — universe. There is nothing else. All variation is in the eye of the gullible.

The cut-outs disappear.

JOE: My parents, though...fuck...I still have issues with them, don't I? Sheesh. Anyway, they were raised to fear, and yet adore God. Judgment was always coming. Punishment, wrath, but when you were feeling blue, God had a shoulder to cry on. I like wrath, but come on. I'd say, "They can whip me, they can spit on me, they can crucify me, but I'll never pretend to believe!" We used to fight about it all the time because we didn't have a TV. They wouldn't allow it. See?...My irregular parents would often stand outside the bathroom door while I was in the shower and shout that there had to be something out there, someone at the helm, a protector. I'd say, "Read your horoscope, ya fuckin' idiots! Science is still the history of dead religions." Of course, secretly, I wanted to believe...but like many of you, I could not make the leap without laughing.

Besides, people who have to remind you every few minutes of how righteous and holy they are always have something to hide. Not some of the time. All of the time. All of them. All of the time... I'm an open book. Sadly, it's a book no one can read... maybe we're only here now because something like us fed us once too often. But here's my point — didn't we decide everything from there? Didn't somebody decide? Didn't we sit there and watch someone decide? Well, didn't we? Didn't we sit quietly and watch somebody take us to this? Hmmmmmmm ... am I ever stoned... sorry... how are you quacks doin'? Is that a little tight on the wrists?... Doesn't look too comfortable ... (*to someone off*) They'll need their hands for the paperwork!

Sound: A harp plays sweetly. Joe sits, drinks.

JOE: God and his dog are asleep behind the barn. Mid-morning on the farm. His red plaid spring jacket, yellow hair turning white in the sun. Mother is calling him and the birds are just calling. God's dog sleeps at his master's feet, curled up and still. He sleeps close for warmth. But from a distance God's dog could be a stone. Curling up to be a rock is a survival instinct. If a lion attacks, it might grab one of the others while you haul ass.

Music out.

JOE: Lets dance! Hey! That was great! I think the show's really picking up! See, I'm fun! I'm just a big fuckin' bag of fun a hundred percent of the time!... This could go on, you know ... for days... think of how easy it would be to record a simple statement regarding my mental health... a bit of video, a piece of paper... what's all the fuss about? What's wrong with you people?... Gordon, my mother's slam, ate a bunch of mushrooms one night and went on for like way longer than I have up to this point, about time, and how like time is like moving and like it's all moving forward right, even for like bugs, and, you know, dirt and like the things that live in the dirt. Time goes forward, but we don't, right? We're a baby, right? We're always mostly like the baby who, like, goes into the woods and just stares at his own reflection in a pool. And he's like so fucking struck, right, by his own image that he doesn't come when they call to him... and then it gets dark.

It gets dark. The faint light across his face is fractured. There is a long silence as he moves forward, slowly, stopping to look over his shoulder.

JOE: Rats...

He is now downstage. He regards the audience as his accomplice. Everything's cool.

JOE: Okay. As soon as the door clicks. Soon as you hear the click. You just swing the fuckin' crowbar with everything you got. All right? Get comfortable... breathe slowly... deep breaths, Gordon... don't think about anything... you okay?... Okay.

As his light fades, it appears as though he has been stabbed from behind. Beat. His light returns.

JOE: Gord doesn't remember a thing... of course, he does remember. But he believes that he doesn't... so he doesn't... that's Gord-o logic. It's Gord-o magic. Whenever we'd get drunk he'd start whining about Philip. "You gotta tell me what happened, man... tell me what happened at the lake. I don't remember anything." Fuckin' born hypnotized... Gord-o loves a pan fried trout. He'll do anything for ya. Diane — my reluctant weapons specialist — says, we're afraid to look because our beauty is more terrible than our thoughts. Our secret beauty is soft and oily, smeared across cosmic memory. I can say things like *cosmic memory* with a straight face because I don't have a problem with being unintentionally funny. I get mocked a great deal and I'm always relieved. I'm a cool loner. I'm cool. I'm modern! You can be, too! On the big day, you'll get a notice to take your poor children out of school. You'll be instructed as to where you should go to collect your optional uniform and mandatory beach towel. Volunteers will go door to door, collecting cell phones and weapons. Anything that needs charging. Otherwise, everybody gets what they need. Everybody gets what they want — within reason — and it's all free. Absolutely free, no money down...no money.

He winks at us.

JOE: People will line the streets by the millions, all over the world, anxious to be one of us. There'll be no more of this nonsense and you won't miss any of it. I often ask myself, when I'm pretending to be interviewed, why you? How did Joe get to this profound state of enlightenment? Why you and not anyone else? And I answer...because...something's got to happen. Someone has to be the decider. I believe it should be someone who's never been in the big chair before. A regular Joe like me ...Philip used to talk like a regular Joe. He was good at that. He knew all the words. Knew how to infiltrate on a social level. That's how he did his work...you know, in retrospect, we only hated each other for political reasons...and maybe that's part of why I no longer tolerate politics. I'm saving lives. And let's face it...we're stuck here. I have a good friend at Interpol who trades information for vintage pornography from the turn of the century. Three years ago, he told me that — realistically — complete world domination can be sketched out in Nine Steps. If he's right, I'm at Step Seven. Of course, I could be lying...I suppose. But then, what difference would that make? My right-hand men could be lying to me as well. I could be leading them down the garden path...but what's wrong with going to the garden? And if my right-hand men want to keep their right hands, they'll stay the course...I'm kidding, obviously. They're on side. They're ready to rock!... Let's rock! Look — sometimes the bad guy is the only one who knows a way out of the burning building...and the fucking hero has no choice but to take the cuffs off him...and I've made no secret of my mistakes. Not that I think killing Philip was a mistake. I don't. It wasn't even my first try.

Sound: A meandering, acoustic guitar plays sweetly.

JOE: The first attempt I made on Philip's remarkable life was after a dance one night. Everybody was really drunk. Everybody but me, of course... I gave Gord the crowbar. We stood in the dark hall and waited. Philip was on to us, though. I don't know how, exactly, but it hardly matters now. He came in through a window. Stuck me in the back with a spike. He was a little skittish for a long time after that. I wasn't afraid of him at all because people who talk big never do anything. I played him casually, but carefully. He wasn't completely stupid... when they make the movie of my life, Tom Cruise is going to play him and I'm going to play myself. Anyway...

We hear a gunshot. Then someone crying out in pain as glass shatters and filing cabinets topple in the distance. There is another shot, closer.

JOE: Listen... no one — *listen*. No one is going to hurt you... there's nothing to be afraid of... all I want from you is an honest decision, an official seal of approval on my walkin' papers... and just — on a personal note — if you think I'm unfit... that's only because you're too weak... to make a simple leap of faith... and understand this, unless you come to the right decision... I'll have no time for you... I can't promise any kind of protection... I can't promise you anything. "Is it really over, Brad?" Watch out — "C'mon, Tasha. Let's go home. That motorcycle driving prick is burning in Hell with all of our enemies whose stomachs have probably exploded by now and whose liquefied brains have shot out of their nostrils like snot by NASA and whose ways were wicked and wrong and weak and whose torment is unimaginable." "Is it really over, Brad?" "Yeah, Trophy. It's all over. It's all over now."

Blackout. Sound: Loud, symphonic, anthem-like music. It must not have any political affiliation. A bright light strobes on a heavily decorated podium. Joe appears behind it, smiling and waving. An enormous tangle of streamers falls all over the stage. His voice is slightly distorted by the hot mic. As the music fades out, Joe motions to the empty area downstage. The lighting becomes an unstable wash of yellowish white light. The anthem distorts as it fades.

Joe looks off.

JOE: Give them a hand!

A bloody severed hand is tossed to the centre of the stage. Three or four more land beside it.

Sound: A big, realistic cheer.

JOE: Seriously... I want to thank each and every one of you for coming out to see me live.

Sound: Another cheer.

JOE: You know, in the woods, you keep to yourself and hope that nothing eats you. If something tries, you should fight back, even if you've been told not to.

Sound: A bigger cheer. In it we hear garbled bits of the show as before. Silence.

JOE: As you download your day, I want you to think about gravity. I want everyone with an even number between ten million and eight hundred million to think extremely negative thoughts about the Eastern Resistance.

Sound: An even bigger cheer. Under it, there is more screaming and more intense animal growls.

JOE: Try to imagine them being discovered and arrested. Imagine clubbing the shit out of those ungrateful, backward assholes on our behalf.

Sound: Again, a big cheer, screaming, and more intense animal growls.

JOE: For the next three days, I want everyone with an odd number between four billion and five billion, to invent a new musical instrument that anybody can play. The best one will win a prize!

Sound: Another big cheer. Under it, more screaming, more intense animal growls and a meat saw at work.

JOE: Also, I want Ireland to stay awake tonight. So, if you're in Ireland, do not... do *not* fall asleep until the sun comes up. I need you to stay up.

A star field forms over the theatre. Pause.

JOE: There's... a bad element... there are people out there who still have no idea... this is not a temporary situation! No one is going to come through the ceiling with guns blazing to save anybody's sorry ass from me... this is it... the standards have officially gone up... but there's a bad element out there ... they want to take our standards back down to where they've been for a thousand years... they want your life to be about standing still... and then slowly drifting backwards... back into the shit... they want you safely smothered in poisonous tradition and common sense. Well, see if you don't agree when I say, it's time to fuck them!

Sound: Another cheer. Under it, chaos.

JOE: But enough shoptalk. Here's this week's dividend: Say, look up at the stars! Are you looking at the stars? If you're curious about becoming famous, sign up before your next birthday to be a celebrity. If today is your birthday, fuck you. You're getting more than enough attention, aren't you?

Sound: Cheering and chaos. This fades gradually as the anthem plays.

JOE: BLAH BLAH BLAH BLAH BLAH BLAH BLAH. Something else you want to hear. BLAH BLAH BLAH BLAH. Yadda yadda, etcetera.

Joe tips the podium and it collapses into a bed of exotic flowers. He stands on the green mound in the middle of it. A shaft of milky white light hits him. His dancing goons enter without their tutus. One has an assault weapon over her shoulder. They are waving large, white silky flags. The goons march back and forth as Joe stares off, steel-eyed. After a few crosses, the goons lie on the floor and cover themselves with their flags. They die.

Sound: A low electric hum fades in as the anthem distorts and fades out. The lights fade, leaving a dim, bluish haze. Joe moves slowly to centre stage.

Sound: A distant gunshot. Pause. A distant burst of machine gun fire. Joe thinks for a moment, almost laughs. He stares at the floor. There is a long silence. Sound: The last cheer at mid-point. It's jarring. Simultaneously, all of the lights return at their full intensity. They go out as the sound stops, abruptly. As this brief cut of the cheer plays, Joe's hands shoot upwards and he throws his head back, ready for lightning.

THE END.

DEAD
MEAT

DEAD MEAT

Lights rise on a police station waiting room. Flo Mulls sits, waiting, her knapsack on her lap. She is in her mid-thirties. There is an almost visible cloud of melancholy around her.

The music fades.

Warren Hayes enters. He is her age. He wears a conservative suit. He is as bewildered as he is angry.

WAR: Is it me?

FLO: Let's not, okay?

WAR: Are you mad at me, Flo? Is that —

FLO: I don't know any more now —

WAR: Cuz...

FLO: —than I did before.

WAR: This is —

FLO: I don't learn anymore.

WAR: It just isn't normal.

FLO: Well, compared to what?

WAR: WHAT THE FUCK, Flo?

FLO: I'm sorry!

WAR: Yeah.

FLO: (*almost smiles*) I am.

WAR: How come you never sound sorry when you're saying it?

FLO: I don't know anything, Warren.

WAR: Don't f—

He turns away because he wants to strangle her. Silence.

FLO: I think maybe they have to make me over. Shrinks or better pills or... what are you thinking?

WAR: I was fantasizing about strangling you.

FLO: Really?

WAR: Yes.

Pause.

FLO: I'm sorry.

She thinks for a moment, eyes on the floor. She smiles. Warren turns to study her. Pause.

WAR: And why can't you at least steal something normal? Like a normal thief? What's so exciting about the fucking butcher's shop?

FLO: Don't swear at me. I hate that.

WAR: But it keeps me from murdering you, Hon!

FLO: Violent thoughts are as bad as violent actions, Warren.

WAR: Are they? Why steaks?

FLO: I don't —

WAR: Don't say you don't know. Just tell me — now... Why'd you steal the tenderloins, Flo?... Were ya hungry?... Cuz...

Speechless, he shakes his head in disbelief. She smiles at him. Pause.

WAR: It's not funny anymore.

FLO: I am sorry.

WAR: I want an answer. Now!

FLO: I'm telling you, I don't know. I think... maybe they can give me shock treatment or something. That's back in vogue. And apparently it's a lot nicer now... I think about the strangest things.

WAR: Why didn't ya just pay for the meat?

FLO: I wanted to pay for it. I wanted to... but the butcher was this — big, muscle-bound — gym rat guy... big super hero arms, you know. And I wanted to see...

Pause. She thinks.

WAR: What?

Pause. She doesn't want to tell him, now.

FLO: I wanted to see if he could catch me. (*off his look*) Because he was weighed down with all that extra flesh! The big man boobs and (*indicates huge thighs*)... I thought I could outrun him. You don't know, I'm really fast on the treadmill now.

WAR: Holy shit, Flo... ya don't make it easy, do ya?

FLO: I'm —

WAR: Don't say you're sorry. You're not sorry. You just wanna punish me for something. I don't know what. But it's childish. It's bullshit.

FLO: I didn't plan to get caught!

WAR: That's not the point! You have no reason to steal anything! ...You have no reason to bark at our neighbours.

FLO: That was weeks ago.

WAR: You have no reason to wear that stupid turban when you walk the dog.

FLO: I swear to god, she won't poop if I don't wear the turban. I can't help that. That's nature. And nature does not give the smallest of shits about what we want.

WAR: I'm tired of the jokes and — and the comments — from everybody. We're a joke. Even your lunatic family can see that what we have together is a really old — fucking old, tired joke. And it's not funny anymore.

FLO: Why do you hate my family?

WAR: I'm pretty sure that's the other way around.

FLO: They don't hate you. They just can't get past your defenses. No one can.

WAR: What?

FLO: You're very defensive. You're rigid. At least I try to have fun.

WAR: This is fun?... Why have you started stealing, Flo?... (*with unchanging inflection*) Why?... Why?... Why?... Why?... Why?... Why?... Why?

FLO: I don't know angry robot. I'm stumped.

WAR: Fucking say it.

FLO: Okay! The truth is...

Pause. She thinks.

FLO: It just happens, sometimes... no matter where I am or who I'm with... I feel like I'm just — observing everything... from a long way away.

Pause. She dreads her own words.

FLO: And I see — how separate I am — from everything... and it's so — empty on my side of the world... then I steal something. Lately meat, but that's only my fixation on the butcher. I hope his name is Butch.

WAR: You know what?

FLO: I don't know anything.

WAR: Sometimes I see myself as being separated from the world, too, because that's what everybody feels sometimes. And I don't steal shit... you got it pretty good. Better than most. So it — it begs the question, why... Why?... Why?

FLO: Here's a — okay, here's a question for you. For what, Warren, am I supposed to feel guilty?

WAR: Who said anything about guilt?

FLO: Every time you say my name — I feel like — like I'm being prepped for surgery.

WAR: That's — great.

FLO: Like you're trying to cure me of something, but what you see as this terrible disease — is just me.

WAR: I only wanna know about your new stealing hobby. What's it really about? And don't say the empty room or anything about who can run the fastest, cuz that's just weak.

Pause. She considers him for a moment.

FLO: It's not new... I'm just getting caught, lately... When I was twelve, I stole a Persian cat from the big-headed girl, three streets over. Lots of stuff at every school, right through college.

WAR: What?

FLO: Just before I met you, I stole almost the entire Cheeses of the World display from the Borsky Deli. One piece at a time. I took a pound of it out of there every month. Under my sweater.

WAR: What the fuck are you telling me?

FLO: But I got caught.

WAR: What?

FLO: Cuz who's pregnant for eleven months, right? I tried to give the cheese back, but... they didn't want it.

Pause. She notices him suddenly regarding her with suspicion.

FLO: What?

WAR: What do you mean your fixation on the butcher?

FLO: What?

WAR: You said you had a fixation on that butcher.

FLO: I just think I can outrun him.

WAR: Right... why won't you just say it? Get it over with.

FLO: What are you talking —

WAR: You're done with me... that's what it is... and whether you did it before or not, the stealing is just another — distraction. To keep me away... you don't have the guts to say it. You're a chicken.

FLO: A chicken?

WAR: A coward.

FLO: Am I?

WAR: Yeah. Go fuck the butcher.

FLO: What'd I say?!

WAR: You're already way past the point when you could have saved it.

FLO: Oh, come on, ya big —

WAR: All you had to do was deny it right away.

FLO: Deny what?

WAR: You deserve one of those beefy fucks who lives at the gym and thinks about his ass muscles all day. You're juvenile.

FLO: You're certifiable. I just wanted a little excitement.

WAR: With the young, muscle-bound butcher.

She explodes.

FLO: I'm dying of boredom, you critical mutherfucker!

Pause. She takes a breath and then bends at the waist as though she might make him airborne with a final blast of her voice.

FLO: FUUUUUUCK OOOOFFFFFF!!!

She straightens, a little amazed at herself. Pause. A uniformed cop, Dutch, enters. He's a friendly, square-jawed, burly man of about forty-five.

DUTCH: How's every little thing in here?

Pause. Warren stares at Flo. She summons her acting skills, points at Warren.

FLO: He tried to strangle me.

WAR: Don't even —

DUTCH: Is this true?

WAR: No! Nothing she says is true! You all know that by now.

DUTCH: Calm down.

FLO: Please stay, Officer. I don't want to be alone with him.

WAR: You're so fucking —

DUTCH: Hey!

WAR: —fucked in the head.

DUTCH: Hey, hey. Calm down, sir. Did you physically assault your wife?

WAR: No.

FLO: He has a record.

DUTCH: Let him talk, please, Ma'am.

FLO: (*pointing at Warren*) Street angel, house devil. Right there!

DUTCH: Why don't you go get yourself a coffee while I talk to your husband?

FLO: I'd like to go home, if that's all right.

DUTCH: Bail's paid. You can go if you'd like.

WAR: Jeez, Flo, you should get a Daytime Emmy for this one.

FLO: You're a bully!

DUTCH: That's enough, now.

WAR: Just go.

Flo pretends to be fighting back tears.

FLO: I hope you don't come home too angry, Warren... I don't think I can outrun you.

She starts out.

WAR: Holy shit.

At the exit, unseen by the Dutch, Flo dances like a jerk for a second or two and smiles broadly at Warren. He watches her, indifferently. Exit Flo.

DUTCH: Sometimes you want to turn to smoke and drift away on the air. All the time, for you, maybe. Not me, though. I wanna be wood. A wooden man... anyway. She's getting better.

WAR: I don't care.

DUTCH: You wish that was true.

WAR: I don't see what's better about her.

DUTCH: She tried to get caught this time. So maybe the novelty's wearin' off. She certainly didn't get much of a chase from him.

WAR: How's that?

DUTCH: That old butcher would have keeled over if he dialed the phone too fast.

WAR: Oh, yeah?

DUTCH: We should all be so lucky to live that long, my friend. They've got a tree in British Columbia that's thirteen-hundred years old. Douglas fir.

Warren nods. Pause.

WAR: I could sleep for a year.

DUTCH: You wanna turn to smoke and drift away.

WAR: What?

DUTCH: Not me. I wanna be rooted in the soil — you know, out in the wind, soaking up the sun...a wooden man with hundreds of fingers reachin' up and up and up...that'll always be my goal, I guess. Sorry. My wife says I take too many pills for too many things I don't have.

WAR: I know, Dutch. Thanks for not charging her.

DUTCH: What are friends for?

WAR: I owe you.

DUTCH: I know.

Enter Flo.

FLO: Excuse me, Officer.

DUTCH: Hello, there.

FLO: I'd like to apologize.

Dutch and Warren exchange a glance.

FLO: He didn't try to strangle me. I just made that up because I'm — you know — crazy.

DUTCH: Crazy in love.

FLO: Yeah.

DUTCH: I understand. Everybody makes mistakes. My wife, Estelle, says "Nobody's good at anything." Doesn't seem fair, but that's Estelle. She's unfair. You folks have a terrific day.

WAR: We sure will.

FLO: Thanks a lot.

DUTCH: Just doin' my job ma'am.

Exit Dutch. Warren and Flo consider each other.

FLO: I am sorry.

He stares at her, unmoved.

WAR: No, you're not.

FLO: No. Not really. But it's nice of me to want to say so.

WAR: Listen... I want you to not steal anything for a year.

FLO: Good luck with that.

WAR: And stay away from that butcher.

FLO: Oh, come on.

WAR: I mean it.

FLO: You're being ridiculous. Boys that age don't have the depth to appreciate a woman of my — you know, all my shit... whatever. Let's get out of here.

They start out. She stops, sniffs the air, winces a bit.

FLO: You notice that?

WAR: What?

FLO: That smell.

WAR: What smell?

FLO: Dead meat... it smells like the first day of school... or like the hospital you die in... something final.

WAR: I suppose.

Pause. She considers him.

FLO: If we did love each other... and if all of this were real... or important... it would be much more painful, wouldn't it?

Pause. He considers her.

WAR: Just stay away from the butcher.

FLO: All right... but this is what we're going to do... we're going to have a little race... if you get to the corner before me, we stay married... if I get there first, we have a divorce... a big, ugly, loud, expensive, hilarious divorce...'K?... Okay?... You ready?

He nods.

WAR: I'm ready.

FLO: Get set... GO!

Exit Flo, running. Warren watcher her go. He sighs. He sits. He stares.

THE END.

SMOKE & BLOOD

SMOKE AND BLOOD

Rome, 55 BC. A garden.

Lucretius is seated on a stone bench, hunched over. The shawl of his toga is wrapped around his waist, hiding an uncomfortable erection. He sighs deeply. He's forty-four years old. Decius, an ambitious man of about thirty, enters with a goblet in hand. Slashes of moonlight fall over them, a raucous party goes on in the nearby house. Through much of the din, a male voice is barking one-liners at a receptive crowd.

DECIUS: You weren't supposed to drink that one, Lucretius.

LUCRETIUS: No shit.

DECIUS: (*whispers loudly*) Vitellius Pius is here.

LUCRETIUS: I don't know who that is.

DECIUS: Vitellius Pius? He could be a senator — and sooner than anyone thinks.

LUCRETIUS: So?

DECIUS: Well — we all aren't poets, Lou. We mortals have to kiss some ass now and again.

Lucretius holds himself, winces.

LUCRETIUS: Poets live like mice. It's worse now than when I first drank the philter. Fuck!

DECIUS: Did you whack off?

LUCRETIUS: (*disgusted*) Twice.

DECIUS: Well, it can't stay up forever.

LUCRETIUS: It can! And it does! This could last another ten or twelve hours... unless I stop my heart.

DECIUS: Right... well... it's a pretty good party, though.

LUCRETIUS: I'm going to kill myself.

DECIUS: It's nothing to be embarrassed about. You know, you really shouldn't have run out here like that. You looked crazy.

LUCRETIUS: I am crazy!

DECIUS: Well. You shouldn't let people see it.

LUCRETIUS: Of course, I'm crazy. I've wasted my life writing a poem... while the riots exploded all over Rome, I was pecking at a piece of parchment... like a hungry gull... on a wooden mackerel. Fuck, I'm terrible.

DECIUS: Yeah, well.

LUCRETIUS: While the wars raged...

DECIUS: You were writing a —

LUCRETIUS: I was mulling over useless words. For what?

DECIUS: (*shrugs*) You revere Epicurus. You're keeping his ideas alive. Protesting. And it's funny. You're funny.

LUCRETIUS: But what's it for?

DECIUS: I don't know. Love? You love Epicurus, maybe.

LUCRETIUS: He's been dead for a couple of hundred years, Darius.

DECIUS: *Decius.*

LUCRETIUS: Decius.

DECIUS: I don't mean love like that. I mean, you respect him, even though you've never known him. You're making him famous again.

LUCRETIUS: I'll never finish it.

DECIUS: You have a purpose. You're keeping his thoughts alive in a way that modern people can relate to. It's important.

LUCRETIUS: I'm forty-four years old and I've accomplished nothing. I want to die.

DECIUS: Lucretius. Shut the fuck up. You haven't been poisoned … the joke was supposed to be on Flavius. It's no big deal.

LUCRETIUS: Go back inside. Kiss some ass.

DECIUS: Anyone else would just take advantage of the situation. You should go to the baths. *(Lucretius scoffs)* Go to the baths, meet some whores and forget about the world. There'll still be a war to protest tomorrow and every other tomorrow.

LUCRETIUS: Then I should die tonight.

DECIUS: Listen — he wasn't no poet, but here's the way my old man used to say it: War is in our nature. Accept it.

LUCRETIUS: No. No. It's not natural. Blood lust is a symptom of a disease. The fact that it exists doesn't make it normal.

DECIUS: But there are two sides to every —

LUCRETIUS: All sorts of abnormal things exist. And everything has many more sides than two.

DECIUS: But men have always fought for —

LUCRETIUS: Evil is the refusal of awareness, Decius. And Rome refuses to be aware of the cruelty that pays for our gluttony.

DECIUS: Look. Everyone doesn't have your —

LUCRETIUS: Everyone starts out the same. Then we're told, over and over — by a tiny handful of the sickest ones — that the illness is normal... the infection isn't merely fashionable like it is in Rome. It's desirable, now. Everywhere.

DECIUS: But so many of us want to make war —

LUCRETIUS: So many? A tiny minority. Mutants. They seduce young men with the romance of carnage. They do it for fame and gold. To live on a coin for a few generations. Or a few months.

DECIUS: Well, old men can't fight in wars.

LUCRETIUS: They can. But they don't have to. Any one of these men you pretend to admire would gladly wage war for Rome, because they're never in any danger.

DECIUS: It's just what we are, Lucretius.

LUCRETIUS: What *they* are — that tiny few — is a nest of snakes. They're spreading the plague of the empire — far and wide. To smother the world in it.

DECIUS: We are rescuing barbarians who live in total ignorance.

LUCRETIUS: Yes. Ignorance of our knowledge. And we're only saving the few we don't enslave or kill.

DECIUS: Sometimes there's no choice. Sometimes it's the will of Mars.

LUCRETIUS: Oh, it's always the gods with you assholes! And since the holy generals all believe that we're on the verge of the end of the world, they have nothing to lose. The rest of us just have to duck. Oh, Fuck!

He grips his throbbing erection, leans forward a little.

DECIUS: Go to the baths, Lou.

Enter Vitellius Pius. He's rich and pompous. He wears a garland on his right shoulder. His toga is expensive: white, trimmed in purple. He has thrown the shawl over his left shoulder. He's a little drunk. He's about thirty-eight.

VITELLIUS: Decius — orphaned by the gods!

DECIUS: Vitellius!

Vitellius gives Decius a paternal kiss on the forehead.

VITELLIUS: (*noticing Lucretius*) I suppose I don't have to ask who drank the cock philter.

DECIUS: Vitellius Pius, this is Titus Lucretius Carus.

VITELLIUS: It's a pleasure. Don't get up.

Vitellius laughs, so Decius follows suit.

VITELLIUS: Sorry.

DECIUS: Lucretius, where's your sense of humor?

LUCRETIUS: Um — I'm a poet?

VITELLIUS: I'm sorry about the mix-up, honestly. Your cup was meant for Marcus Flavius as a birthday joke. I should have been paying closer attention.

DECIUS: There were many cups on the table. It was an easy mistake.

VITELLIUS: You know, I read some of your poem "On the Nature of Everything."

LUCRETIUS: "On the Nature of Things."

VITELLIUS: Either way, I didn't understand it. I think you've got a lot of work ahead of you on that one.

LUCRETIUS: That one is the only one and maybe you should go—

VITELLIUS: What was the line about the mind and the body and—

DECIUS: "The body searches for that which has injured the mind with love." I know it backwards and forwards.

LUCRETIUS: It's better forwards, I think.

VITELLIUS: The body searches...

DECIUS: "The body searches for that which has injured —

VITELLIUS: For that which has injured —

DECIUS: — the mind with love."

VITELLIUS: "The body searches for that which has injured the mind with love"… "The body searches — for that which has injured the mind… with love."

Vitellius thinks for a moment, laughs.

VITELLIUS: What — in the name of all of the Emperor's bastard sons — is that supposed to mean?

Decius laughs, heartily.

VITELLIUS: That's why you're still so obscure, my friend.

DECIUS: (*to* Lucretius) He's kidding.

VITELLIUS: Poets muddy the water. Don't they? Poetry is mud.

LUCRETIUS: Why don't you go fuck yourself.

VITELLIUS: Pardon me?

LUCRETIUS: I said, why —

DECIUS: He's in pain. From the erection. And he's a little bold from the wine. He doesn't mean any disrespect.

VITELLIUS: He means nothing but… I may not see through your mud, but I know what you're up to.

LUCRETIUS: Do ya?

VITELLIUS: You want to drive the gods out of our lives. You want to rule us.

LUCRETIUS: I don't want anything but logic to rule us.

VITELLIUS: Exactly. Where's the fun in that?

DECIUS: I keep telling him —

VITELLIUS: Am I right?

DECIUS: — to loosen up. Yes, you're right. Lucretius, go to the baths.

VITELLIUS: You're fond of old Epicurus, aren't you?

Lucretius studies Vitellius Pius for a moment.

LUCRETIUS: So?

VITELLIUS: My father read every word. And like you, he had bouts of madness. Hallucinations.

Decius and Lucretius are both a little surprised by this jab.

VITELLIUS: It's all right. I understand. That philosophy was a source of hope for him, I think. But it's just another madman's vision, Lucretius. No mind matters that much. And the gods won't be dismissed so easily.

LUCRETIUS: (*to Decius*) "All life is a struggle in the dark."

VITELLIUS: Isn't it considered bad taste to quote oneself?

LUCRETIUS: Ah!

Lucretius smiles for the first time.

LUCRETIUS: Maybe you know my poem backwards and forwards, too.

VITELLIUS: You're an upstart, Lucretius.

LUCRETIUS: I'm a nobody.

Vitellius smiles and nods at Lucretius.

VITELLIUS: "In the midst of the fountain of wit there arises something bitter..."

LUCRETIUS: What is it you want, Vitellius Pius?

VITELLIUS: I'm merely being social.

DECIUS: Sure. We're all friends here. We're all Romans... right?

LUCRETIUS: I give people the option of dealing with reality, instead of wallowing in their sad inheritance, Pius. Superstitious times are bad times for courage.

VITELLIUS: You — are an arrogant fool. De Rerum Natura. You're so sure of yourself. Fuck you and your dead teacher.

LUCRETIUS: You will be dust, Pius. And your words will be lost as quickly as the soldiers you'll hire in the spring.

VITELLIUS: Oh!

LUCRETIUS: Buried like statues in conquered lands.

VITELLIUS: You think so?

LUCRETIUS: My words will never die. Epicurus will never die. Nations will rise and fall... all of the gods will fall to the earth like breathless birds — but the truth is constant. And unmovable.

VITELLIUS: You know, people burn the copies of your rambling poem. It's rambling. The Christians say you're a demon.

Lucretius scoffs.

DECIUS: When he recites, though, it really comes to life. Lucretius is a very passionate man. And maybe some misinterpret him.

VITELLIUS: Is that what I've done?

DECIUS: No! No. No, you —

VITELLIUS: Your poem would be helpful if you weren't in it so much. You are not—listen to this—you are *not* above the gods. You will not live forever.

LUCRETIUS: I won't survive the night.

DECIUS: Oh, come on.

VITELLIUS: I'm sorry to hear that.

LUCRETIUS: But the poem will live for as long as there are people to read it.

DECIUS: I think that much of the glory of Rome comes from it's great artists and I think —

LUCRETIUS: You're afraid. All you know is fear.

VITELLIUS: I fear nothing. Because I have seen into the future. The Fates have spoken to me. Long after we're gone, the empire will thrive. We are supreme... all of the gods in the heavens will protect us — from the likes of you... good night, Lucretius.

Exit Vitellius.

DECIUS: Vitellius...

Decius sighs, considers Lucretius.

DECIUS: Well, you made a very influential enemy, Lucretius.

LUCRETIUS: It doesn't matter. I have only a few hours left in this life. It's a relief.

DECIUS: Oh, stop moaning. You're an old man with clear eyes and a hard-on. To ask for more would be sickening.

LUCRETIUS: Why are you here, Decius?

DECIUS: I'm concerned about you.

LUCRETIUS: No, I mean, why are you here — alive in the world?

Decius scoffs, not sure how to even comprehend the question.

DECIUS: Because the gods gave me to my parents.

LUCRETIUS: You have ambition. You choose this. Over and over — you accept the way things are — the hypocrisy. And you thrive in it.

DECIUS: It was like this when I got here.

LUCRETIUS: But how will it change?

DECIUS: When the gods will it to change, Lucretius.

LUCRETIUS: Oh.

DECIUS: You can't prove they're not up there.

LUCRETIUS: You just did.

DECIUS: No, I didn't.

LUCRETIUS: If they were up there, proof would never be an issue.

DECIUS: The people need them.

LUCRETIUS: The way a condemned man needs a blindfold.

DECIUS: No. The way any living thing needs hope...let me be your friend, Lucretius...come back inside.

LUCRETIUS: Nothing consumed by the toil of living needs hope ...I think the party's over.

DECIUS: Well...maybe you should go home.

LUCRETIUS: Goodbye, Decius.

DECIUS: I'll see you.

LUCRETIUS: You'll see my corpse.

Before Decius can object.

LUCRETIUS: And don't pray for me. Forget me. I'm glad it's over.

Holding the toga's shawl tightly around him, Lucretius makes a weary exit.

DECIUS: I don't want to struggle in the dark, Lou!...Lucretius!

He watches him go for a moment. Exit Decius, back to the party.

Electronic music rises under the din of the party inside. There is more light now, besides the moonlight, with city colours in it.

IDA *leads* **JOE** *to the stone bench. Ida has a small, over-designed backpack and a camera. Joe, a likeable hipster, is twenty-five. He is blindfolded, holding an unlit cigarette. Ida is thirty, sly and hopeful and current. They're both high and happy and a bit out of it.*

JOE: I'm sorry. I have to say no.

Ida exhales a pish sound. She considers him for a moment.

IDA: One picture.

JOE: I'm not comfortable with this kind of —

IDA: Since when?

JOE: It's just not the sort of thing that I'm —

IDA: It's not a sort of thing. It's its own thing.

JOE: Hey, I'm not dissing your thing. I would never do that.

IDA: It might be in vain, but there has to be some kind of resistance, Joe.

JOE: Listen.

IDA: Otherwise, years from now, people will look back at us and think we were all in on it.

JOE: And that's definitely a —

IDA: They'll look back at us the way we look back at cave dudes and their hairy wives.

JOE: Well. In that case, fuck 'em.

IDA: Let me shoot you. Please.

Joe removes the blindfold.

JOE: You said you wouldn't ask me to do this.

IDA: I can't believe you're reacting like —

JOE: I don't belong here. I mean, in this kind of place.

IDA: It's art, Joe. You like art.

JOE: Yeah, art's the shit, totally. But I'm personally not comfortable and way too high for this.

IDA: Let's just pretend you said yes and proceed until you feel you have to stop. Then we can just chat until you're ready to continue. You can have that smoke, maybe.

JOE: I don't smoke.

IDA: Let's begin.

JOE: No. Ida, I'm really not —

IDA: You make me beg so that when you finally say yes, I'll be so incredibly grateful — you imagine, via your dick brain — that I might have sex with you.

JOE: Well. Look at me. I got all this wit...and my porn star good looks.

IDA: I don't know about men anymore.

JOE: What's to know?

IDA: Are they always lying? I mean always?

JOE: Mostly. We're simple. Like, there's only two stages in our lives.

IDA: What are they?

JOE: I don't know. They don't have names.

IDA: If they did, what would they be?

JOE: Little and Big, how the fuck should I know what their names would be? The boys just pretend to be what's expected, for the most part and fantazise about being someone way better. You know, someone who can fly or something.

IDA: Isn't that everybody?

She focuses her camera on him.

JOE: No. Just men. Please put your camera into your anus.

IDA: Why are you suddenly so full of shame? You used to be so free and — and happy.

JOE: Look. I don't get naked on the internet.

IDA: Anymore.

JOE: Anymore. People change.

Pause. She regards him, shakes her head.

IDA: This is not like that. You don't have to get naked.

JOE: I don't want to get painted, either.

IDA: It's not paint. It's powder. It washes right off.

Ida produces a small case containing two makeup sponges, red lip colour and a tin of black powder.

JOE: I hate that shit.

IDA: Look. The makeup is an integral part. Everyone who poses has the same —

JOE: I'm not as weird as I used to be, you know. I'm flirting with Conservatism.

Ida cackles, briefly.

JOE: Or like Libertarianism or some other shit that has — you know — rules. Like Boy Scouts, but for, you know, adults.

IDA: Holy shit.

JOE: Everybody's friendly and they have, like, picnics and shit, maybe. Meetings about — ways to make everybody like us. Potato salad.

IDA: Joe!

JOE: The point is, I feel like I could go on to make a name for myself if I stop doing things like —

IDA: You have a name. Close your eyes.

JOE: (*smiling, closing his eyes*) I thought they were closed. I thought I was just picturing you.

Ida begins the makeup job. She blacks out Joe's eyes. She then makes an angled, wide stroke below his cheek bones to make his face menacing. Sloppily, using a narrow brush, Ida paints Joe's mouth blood red, not stopping when he talks. She paints rills of blood running to his chin.

IDA: What other people think of you is bullshit... I had fun at your birthday party.

JOE: Me too. Can you believe how old I am?

IDA: It's maddening. I like your nerd friends. If you ask me, nerds are the shit.

JOE: My friend Blake thinks you're awesome.

IDA: Blake.

JOE: Thinks you're awesome.

IDA: What did he say, exactly?

JOE: I don't know. But he asked me to describe you in one word and I said, "blood-thirsty."

Ida giggles.

JOE: That's one word, right?

IDA: Yeah, well. Your geeky friend likes me. Big deal. Who doesn't?

They both laugh, loudly, at the huge number.

IDA: These days — I don't know if I'm having a sex life or if I'm just doing experiments. Also, scrotums are ridiculous. I'm sorry, but I hate the little nut pouch. It makes me miss sex with women.

JOE: Scrotums have inner beauty. (*enraged*) Goddamnit!

Joe suddenly puts his cigarette in his mouth and holds a lighter in front of it. Pause. Ida eyes him.

IDA: Do it. Light that fucker up...come on...you'll never quit ...you're too weak...weak and easy to control. Come on, bitch, LIGHT IT!

Joe closes his eyes, sighs deeply.

JOE: I want to. I want to, so much. (*whispers*) Oh, fuck me... cigarettes are fantastic.

He takes it out of his mouth, sighs deeply. He pockets the lighter.

JOE: This is dangerous. Being high makes me want to smoke — and talk and talk and talk. And you actually listen. And remember. It's creepy.

IDA: You wouldn't believe how many hits my site gets now.

JOE: How many? Ten thousand?

IDA: Try a hundred thousand.

JOE: Seriously.

IDA: I have a cult following.

JOE: I don't go online anymore. It's all nothing. You should start selling shit, though.

They laugh.

IDA: Yeah. Aprons and such.

JOE: You could ask for donations.

IDA: I don't need donations.

Pause. Joe smiles at Ida.

JOE: You don't buy into anything — in the entire world. Like it's all one hundred percent bullshit and you absolutely know it.

IDA: That's what makes me cool, ya fuckin' idiot.

JOE: It's not nice to call people stupid.

IDA: Only because it's true.

JOE: Well.

IDA: If it weren't true, it would be bizarre to call people stupid. You'd be perplexed when you heard it. But it's not bizarre. It's true. That's what makes it not nice.

JOE: Sore spot.

IDA: Exactly.

JOE: I think your art makes you angry.

IDA: No. Anger feeds the protest. And the protest happens to take the form of visual art. So chew me.

JOE: You're addicted. You *have* to do this Goddess thing now.

IDA: I'm driven by my ego, Joe.

JOE: Women don't have egos.

IDA: I'm afraid of looking stupid to people who won't be born for another couple of hundred years or so.

JOE: Say (*falsetto*) whaaaaat?

IDA: I might have kids and I don't want some snot-nosed brats, down the road, thinking their great-great-great-great-grandmother was some superstitious monkey with a gun in her purse and a bug-sized brain.

JOE: I'll tell ya, I've been curious about death, lately. Everybody's going to die — so what's the hurry? And who cares what's after? Everything's here. I mean —

He gestures to everything in the world for a moment.

JOE: If this doesn't astonish you, what do you want? Why doesn't everybody stop having hissy fits. It's the hissy fits, isn't it? Everybody needs to fuck so far off — that everybody else looks like ants to them... cuz they've fucked so... far... off.

IDA: I could kiss you, Joe.

JOE: I dare you.

IDA: Aw?

JOE: It's true, though. Everything is here — in this time. That's all we know so far.

IDA: I know. It's the über pearl — before the über swine.

Joe laughs.

JOE: I think everything is spiritually interconnected. And that the mystical shit can only be found in nature.

IDA: Oh, would ya — stop reading those stupid books you read. Mysticism, it's icing on a brick.

Ida is finished with the makeup.

IDA: You look fantastic.

JOE: Thank you. Now what? Wait... FUCK!

Joe puts the cigarette in his mouth, holds the lighter in front of it.

JOE: I'm going to do it.

IDA: You don't have the guts, Mister...Too Scared To Smoke.

JOE: I'm going to suck it down and it's going to cook my lungs — nice and slow. Mmmmmmmmm. Oh, man. (*eyes closed, whispers*) Cigarette.

He closes his eyes, lights the lighter.

IDA: Yeah. It's gonna taste really good. Plus it'll make you smell like you just shit your pants. So, that's a bonus.

He lets the lighter go out.

JOE: I don't care what you say. It loves me. (*whispers*) Man.

He puts the lighter away. He opens his eyes.

JOE: Who am I supposed to be in this picture?

IDA: No one specific.

JOE: Done.

Ida reaches into her backpack and produces a thick, battered, rolled-up cardboard sign and a blonde fright wig. We see the back of the sign as she unrolls it.

IDA: You just hold the sign and try to make your head like a severed head on a slab. You know, like the sign is the slab.

JOE: This is Goth.

IDA: Are you trying to make me puke?

JOE: Well, if it pouts like a duck

IDA: It's not Gothic!

JOE: So I look dead and hold the sign.

IDA: And you're sure you don't want to get naked?

He sighs.

JOE: I just don't think I should. I'm twenty-five years old, now, Ida.

IDA: I know.

JOE: Porn was fine, back —

IDA: (*simultaneously*) It's not porn! And you know it's not.

JOE: —when I didn't expect to live this long, but now it seems like I should start being somebody. You know, somebody specific who chooses not to whip it out so much.

Pause. Ida considers him.

IDA: If you remember nothing else, remember this when you come down... and really think about it... identity — is a perversion. It's a hell of a lot more perverted than anything you ever could have done on Frat Boy Action dot com.

JOE: How could having an identity be —

IDA: It's about a hundred times worse than crack.

JOE: How so?

IDA: Take your shirt off.

JOE: Seriously, I'm not comfortable with —

IDA: Oh, come on. You've seen my site. You've seen the gallery.

JOE: Well.

IDA: Have you never seen my site? The Goddess is Dead? You've never seen it?

JOE: I don't go online anymore. I have a sex addiction.

IDA: (*laughing*) No, you don't.

JOE: I don't know what that means. The goddess is dead.

IDA: Well. My stupid theory — which is wrong and bad and wrong — is that the goddess being dead is the root of virtually everything that's bad and wrong with everything everywhere. Without the goddess, there's no balance in the world.

JOE: Oh. The feminine side type of thing.

IDA: But the feminine in dreamland.

JOE: Okay.

IDA: Men can't see themselves. And misogyny is pretty much demanded by the whole mental culture. So.

JOE: I used to think misogyny was the study of massage.

Ida sighs.

IDA: Goddess is just the word I use for feminine energy in the world. Anyway, I know I can't change anything in my time. I'm not stupid. This is for the Jetsons type kids, down the road, who find it in the rubble somewhere.

JOE: It could all change during our life.

IDA: We haven't evolved quickly enough.

JOE: Everything changes.

IDA: Well, the bottom line for me is that if we're going to live in a superstitious society and people dig that, I'm like, whatev. But if that's the way it's going to be, we could at least base it on a story where there are two heroes. I don't know — Gobby and Nona? — and they live on a cloud or something. But one is a boy and one is a girl. And they're equally scary and equally nice.

JOE: Nona should have tits all the way around. Like eight of them. And Gobby should have giant nuts. And she can swing on them.

IDA: Straight dudes would never let them exist.

JOE: Men are dicks, lady.

IDA: If there were no more straight men, could you imagine the war shortage?

JOE: Well, I don't think most dudes want —

IDA: The ones you know, Joey. People see what they're conditioned to see. God is a man. And power is the threat of violence.

JOE: Okay. Okay. But putting these pictures on your site — how does that —

IDA: The Jetsons type kids of the future will be digging at the site of what used to be a landfill and they'll find a hard drive with all of the Dead Goddess pictures on it. Then they'll take it home where their Grandmother, who likes to tinker with that sort of artifact, will manage to download the pictures.

JOE: Okay.

IDA: Hard drives will be like landfill oysters.

JOE: You're so high, you're turning see through.

IDA: Not everyone will have a pearl, but some will. They might find my pearl in one of them and then they'll see these pictures and think I must have been awesome.

JOE: Oh.

IDA: So, do you see how it would be better if you got naked for it?

JOE: Don't make me do that. I mean, I wanna help you impress the Jetsons and everything... but I'm just not comfortable being naked in front of a camera.

IDA: Anymore.

JOE: Anymore.

IDA: The shirt, at least.

JOE: Okay.

He takes his shirt off. And she hands him the wig.

IDA: Awesome. And put this on.

He puts on the wig.

IDA: Now hold the sign up and look nice and dead.

Joe holds the sign up to his chin and then "rests" his head on it. His face dies. The sign reads "THE GODDESS IS

DEAD." *The words are written in bold, distressed letters. There is a pale, sickly green background and stains all over the crude banner. Ida crouches to shoot Joe.*

IDA: Severed head on a slab. Crouch a little.

He does so.

IDA: Hold that.

Pause. Several flashes. The distant party din contains a lot of laughter now.

IDA: Perfect.

Joe lowers the sign, takes off the wig.

JOE: You have something to take this stuff off my face?

IDA: Yeah.

Ida goes to her makeup kit, produces a cloth. Joe holds his cigarette, nervously. She cleans the black stripes on his cheeks and then his eyes.

IDA: You're actually shy with your pants on.

JOE: I told you, I'm changing. I'm becoming something.

IDA: You already did, Joey. Long ago... don't fuck it up now.

She wipes his mouth, focusing on it. He watches her eyes. Finally, he drops the cigarette and kisses her passionately. After a few moments, almost unable to support himself, Joe kneels and embraces Ida, pressing his face into her. She smiles.

IDA: Joe?

JOE: (*tearfully*) Yeah.

IDA: How long since you had a cigarette?

JOE: Eleven days!

Pause. He weeps. Ida strokes his hair, lovingly.

IDA: Do you have condoms?

He looks up at her and smiles.

JOE: Yes!

He stands.

JOE: Yes, I do.

She blindfolds him.

IDA: Okay, Joe. It's on. But this goes down my way.

She leads him, chuckling, off the stage. The party sound fades, the lights change back to moonlight.

Decius enters. He's drunk.

DECIUS: Lucretius?... Are you home? Lou?

Decius sits.

DECIUS: You were wise to get away when you did. Flavius insulted Pius and now he's bleeding all over the street (*quietly*) I don't...

He sighs.

DECIUS: Are you sleeping? Lou?

Lucretius enters. He's sweating, clearly having trouble discerning what's real and unreal.

LUCRETIUS: Who's here?

DECIUS: It's me.

LUCRETIUS: Who are you?

Decius scoffs, sadly.

DECIUS: You're as drunk as me.

LUCRETIUS: If you're a demon, you're wasting —

DECIUS: I'm not a demon.

LUCRETIUS: No fear, no pretense.

DECIUS: I'm nothing like a demon.

LUCRETIUS: No fear.

DECIUS: I don't like it.

LUCRETIUS: No pretending. The vessel breaks and the contents dissipate.

DECIUS: I don't.

LUCRETIUS: That's all. I have nothing for you… There's no real warmth in words… burning them only makes you colder.

Pause. Lucretius focuses on Decius as his sobbing subsides.

LUCRETIUS: Can I tell you something?

DECIUS: I'm a coward.

LUCRETIUS: I can see now. It's as though I've been blind since birth... The philter was a mixture of two. One for the body and one for the mind. But the mixture of them both — with my wine... had an effect — unexpected — and now I can see.

DECIUS: Why am I here?

LUCRETIUS: No reason. I can see that there is a code. There's a language. It works, blindly, to replicate itself. And we are only it's vessel. A result, but not a goal.

DECIUS: Lucretius.

LUCRETIUS: What?

DECIUS: I have no fucking idea what you're talking about. Can you just be a normal guy for a minute? Can you just be my friend and stop... my heart — is pounding. I'm so... it scared me, Lucretius. There was so much blood. And he'll die. Flavius will die... I've seen him for the last time... I don't want to... be here. In Rome. I don't want to be here.

LUCRETIUS: I hardly know you... not that it matters. We're all the same bag of bones.

DECIUS: I thought we were friends.

LUCRETIUS: You decided we were.

DECIUS: So we're not friends?

LUCRETIUS: We are and we are not. Like everyone else.

DECIUS: I thought you were going to kill yourself.

LUCRETIUS: I did... but it's happening very slowly... I'm growing into it.

Decius stands.

DECIUS: Grow faster.

LUCRETIUS: Why did you come here?

DECIUS: I came here... to see my friend. But he's dead.

Lucretius sits.

LUCRETIUS: Slow poisons let us see the change. I might get a look at what's going on.

DECIUS: The end is going on! The end of everything is coming! We won't stop until we drown the world in blood... it's the end, Lucretius. It's the end of everything.

LUCRETIUS: Not everything. The birds will continue without us. The sun rises whether we're looking or not. It rises in places where there are no eyes to see it.

Lucretius takes deep breaths, having trouble holding his head upright.

DECIUS: Lucretius... Lou... what's happening?

LUCRETIUS: The beginning... get out of Rome... and do not follow... cowards follow.

DECIUS: What's happening?

LUCRETIUS: Cowards follow, Flavius.

DECIUS: I'm Decius. Maybe you should be in your bed.

LUCRETIUS: No.

DECIUS: What poison did you drink?

LUCRETIUS: In Rome, every breath is poison.

DECIUS: What poison did you drink?

LUCRETIUS: It's a secret.

DECIUS: I'm taking you inside.

Decius helps Lucretius to stand and leads him off.

LUCRETIUS: I'm starting to see through... I'm waking up.

Exit Decius and Lucretius. The modern music under the din of the party returns, the lighting changes.

Ida enters in her underwear and the blonde wig, running and laughing. Joe enters, barefoot and in his underwear. He's right behind her, yelling Ahhhhhhh! Suddenly out of breath, he leans over, breathing hard.

JOE: Time out.

IDA: There's no time out.

JOE: Seriously, we have to stop.

IDA: The pursuit is the most fun part for me.

JOE: It wouldn't be if you chain-smoked since you were ten.

IDA: Aw.

She approaches him. He springs into action, picking her up and laying her down on the bench. She cackles, screams. He kisses her passionately. She breaks it.

IDA: Wait.

JOE: Dude!

IDA: I want more entertainment.

JOE: What?

IDA: Dance for me.

They laugh.

JOE: No.

IDA: Dance or there's no dessert.

He laughs as she pushes him upward.

IDA: Dance, Big Bang!

JOE: You want a show?

IDA: Yeah. (*putting a foot between his legs*) Shake that.

JOE: You want a show?

IDA: I said, yes! What do you want?

They laugh. Joe begins to dance lasciviously. It's not hard to tell that he has done this before.

JOE: Ya like that one? How about this?

> *A man enters, Ken. He is played by the same actor who played Vitellus Pius. He watches the performance, stone-faced.*

JOE: Oh, you're in for it, now!

IDA: Make me actually want it, baby!

> *She cackles. Laughing, he lies over her and kisses her as before. As he kisses her neck, her head turns and she spots Ken. Ida's confidence is gone, she's a girl in trouble.*

KEN: What are you doing, Ida?

> *She covers herself, afraid to speak.*

KEN: Who are you?

JOE: Who are you, Dude?

KEN: I'm the man who owns this property, dude. That's who I am.

IDA: I didn't mean for this many people to be here.

KEN: Don't waste your breath, Ida. Go inside.

> *Embarrassed, she stands and takes Joe's hand, leading him away.*

KEN: He can stay.

IDA: Leave him alone.

KEN: Go inside. Now. (*to Joe*) You, sit there.

Joe remains standing.

JOE: It's okay. (*to Ida*) I'll see you later.

Exit Ida, running. Ken thinks for a moment.

KEN: What's your name?

JOE: Joe.

KEN: I'm guessing you think you know my daughter fairly well.

JOE: I've known Ida for years.

KEN: But you don't know her. I'm not mad at you, Joe. You're just doing what boys do. Ida has a history of mental illness...and drug abuse. She made us old before our time.

JOE: Ida's great...I love her.

Silence. Ken's mood darkens.

KEN: Do you know the kind of people she associates with?

JOE: Well —

KEN: Drug dealers...perverts...degenerates. She has a friend — not an acquaintance — she has a friend who...

He shakes his head.

KEN: ...he masturbates on camera — on the internet. For money. That's the sort of pervert she seeks out. Degenerates who are willing to feed her...her godlessness.

Pause. Ken is a bit overcome, but only for a moment.

KEN: Are you a Christian, Joe?

Pause. Joe eventually nods.

JOE: Yes... yes, sir, I am.

KEN: But you're not married to my daughter.

JOE: No.

KEN: No... you let your lust control you because your faith is waning. I'm not judging you. That's God's work.

JOE: I'm sorry... I want to be better.

Ken kneels.

KEN: Pray with me.

JOE: What?

Ken takes Joe's hand and pulls him down to his knees. Ken closes his eyes and holds Joe's hand while he prays, silently, moving his lips a little. Joe is at a loss, scanning the area for Ida. Decius enters, weeping. He composes himself and then hold his hands out at his sides, fingers together, palms forward and tilted back, slightly. He then raises his arms and looks upward. His ritual done, he lowers his arms and takes a deep breath. He stares, thinking. He wipes his face. Exit Decius.

Ida enters.

She's dressed. She holds Joe's clothes. She creeps over and mimes a hard punch, points at Ken and then says "Let's go" by gesturing with her head. Joe shakes his head and gestures with his hand, as if to say, "I Can't." She repeats her gestures, faster and with more instance. Joe shakes his head, no. He lowers his head, prays silently.

Exit Ida, amazed.

Ken opens his eyes. He looks at Joe. Feeling the gaze, Joe looks up at Ken. He stands.

KEN: I feel responsible for the damage she's done to you, Joe. Seducing you, probably getting you drugs.

JOE: No. Ida is great. I love Ida.

KEN: But that love is only carnal and physical and human. You need divine love first, Joe.

JOE: I think I should go.

KEN: I think you should stay here. With me.

JOE: Um...

KEN: You said you want to be a better man.

JOE: I do.

KEN: How do you know that our meeting like this isn't God giving you the opportunity to change?

Pause. Joe considers this.

JOE: What would we do?

KEN: Pray. We'll pray together, Joe. And when you're healed, God will give you your mission.

JOE: I don't know.

KEN: "He giveth power to the faint; and to them that have no might he increaseth strength."

JOE: Listen, I have to —

KEN: I'll need your help convincing Ida's friends to leave. I could use some help cleaning up, too.

He smiles and puts his hand on Joe's shoulder.

JOE: Well —

KEN: We have a lot of work to do.

Ken puts an arm around Joe and leads him off.

The party noise fades as theme music rises and the lights change. Barely able to stand and walk, Lucretius slowly makes his way to the bench. He spits out a coin.

Staggering, Ida enters. She is also heading for the bench. They spot each other. Silence. She takes a step forward. Cautiously, she reaches out to touch him to see if he's there. When her hand is about to touch him, he lets out his breath and sinks away from her.

LUCRETIUS: Can you see me?... Can you see me?

Pause. She begins to think he's an hallucination.

IDA: No... I can't see you.

The lights bleed out as they very slowly back away from each other. SFX: The din of the party rises and distorts into a long roar that stops abruptly.

THE END.

THE ESCAPE ARTIST

THE ESCAPE ARTIST

Hank is in his forties, dressed in a tux. He is holding an award. He takes a piece of crumpled paper from his pocket.

HANK: Thank you. I wrote a few things down. Of course, I want to thank the Producer's Association for this great honour. Okay. (*reads*) Television, or The Reverse Eye Toilet — as it was known in covered wagon days — is the highest and most noble achievement of mankind. It has been my honour, lo these many thousands of years, to be some of the grease in the gears of this glorious machine that tells us what to think, who to be, and who to hate. On my journey, I have learned that the secret to a great police drama is having just the right murder of just the right woman — with just the right amount of blood splatter and maggots peppered throughout — to kick off a wild forty-three minute ride full of exposition, mumbling and walking around. It is a delicate art that only a scant few of us "Alpha" or "Genius" producers can comprehend. Even those network guys don't get it!

He holds up the award.

HANK: This is why Satan and all of his cousins could not pry this reminder of my greatness from my cold, dead hand. Dying would be A-okay if we could all live on TV. Am I right? On TV, it would turn out that, underneath it all, I'm not really a sour motherfucker and then I pet a dog or save the orphanage or some shit, instead of dying alone in a booby-trapped farmhouse as I have planned. This great series has given me more than too much money and the right kind of envy inspiring stuff. It has changed me...maybe permanently...now, after twenty years in the game, my tears are piss. If I spit on something, it burns a hole through it. I have a bruise the size of a fucking flapjack on the top of my head from banging it on the ceiling of my own mediocrity...

He turns the page over.

HANK: And yet, I know that we, the molders of humanity, must hold fast to our version of the way things are, lest crazy reality rise up and devour us and take our stuff.

HECKLER: (*off*) Say thank you and sit down, Hank.

HANK: Um. Shut that rotting glory hole you use for a mouth, Jerry, I'm not done. I just want to say that dreams really do come true if you're sneaky enough. And speaking of sneaky, I want to thank my partners in crime, Roger and Sue. What can I say about Roger and Sue?

Hank shakes his head, plays sentimental in a very authentic way.

HANK: The both of you look and smell like something lost in the back of the taxidermy shop. The stench is deafening. I hope to someday read about your sloppy murder-suicide. Thanks for nothing, you illiterate, lazy, untalented, talking bags of vomit. And thanks to you, my peers, for being so bad at what you do that my shit looks passable by comparison. G'night, pylons. (*holds up award*) And thanks for the doorstop.

Hank folds his speech as he leaves with his award.

Blackout.

In a coat and hat, Mel waits, staring out at us. He takes an audible breath and holds it. Finally, he exhales. Hank enters, also in a coat. A laptop case dangles from his arm. Mel is clearly affected by Hank's arrival, but he's playing nonchalant. He smiles at Hank. Hank ignores him. Pause.

MEL: Everybody's talking about your speech last night.

HANK: Yeah?

MEL: Sorry I missed that.

HANK: I think it went over pretty well.

MEL: You deserve that award, you know. You make great TV.

HANK: Oh, for fuck sake, Mel.

MEL: I'm just sayin'...

Silence. They wait.

MEL: I'm still down in news... but I'm ready to go, I think.

HANK: Good. News is where people aspire to be assholes.

MEL: Well... anyway. I like your show.

HANK: Thanks. We're like a family. What's with the elevator?

Pause. Mel sighs deeply.

MEL: Um... you probably know about this already, but George and Anita Reed are having a party on Friday and I thought —

HANK: Listen, Mel. Pick somebody nice, okay?

MEL: It's going to be huge. And they seem like cool people.

HANK: (*laughs*) Cool?

MEL: Well. Nice.

HANK: Do you actually know anything about George and Anita?

MEL: I know they invited me to their party. In the most expensive hotel in the city and I'm —

HANK: About twenty years ago, I knew fucking Anita and that infected genital wart she's married to. I was working at a little affiliate, writing news. They were the big power couple in town — and I do mean *town*.

MEL: You — did news?

HANK: Yes, and if you ever tell anybody that I'll stab you. Listen, Mel. George and Anita are very... conservative, I guess, is the polite way of saying it.

Beat. Mel doesn't get it.

HANK: They don't like sexy or ethnic people... or smart people ... or anyone who isn't white and dead inside.

Mel still doesn't clue in.

HANK: You were invited because they don't know you're queer.

MEL: Are you shittin' me?

HANK: I shit you not.

MEL: Well... they invited a lot people from the network, so —

HANK: Yeah, they always suck ass with the media types. You'll piss yourself when you see them. George always has an appendage around Anita — like he's... slowly digesting her. Or laying eggs, maybe. And Anita always scans the room with her... big old eyeballs... like she's X-raying everything. And George just stands there and farts and farts and farts. They're really cool.

MEL: Well, it's just a party. There'll be a billion people there.

HANK: At least.

MEL: Look. I think you're...

Hank looks at Mel.

HANK: What?... You think I'm what?

MEL: I like you, Hank.

Pause. Hank regards Mel.

HANK: You what?

Mel scoffs.

MEL: Why are you being such a bitch?

HANK: Well, didn't we try this before? I mean —

MEL: But I'm totally different now!

HANK: No, you're not. Look, Mel, don't take this personally. I'm just a crusty old fuck. I'm too bitter to live.

MEL: But not really.

HANK: Really. I don't care about anyone's stupid feelings or — or wishes or thoughts or dumb-ass beliefs — because it's all just a big puddle of — of brain sweat, Mel... nobody should be taken seriously by anyone, anywhere.

MEL: Hank —

HANK: It's not you. I think everyone is an irritating — squealing fucking chimp. Sorry if that sounds a bit harsh.

Pause.

MEL: You're just afraid of rejection.

HANK: Yeah, underneath it all. What do you want, Mel? You want me, in a bad jacket, full of Scotch and as high as fuck —

MEL: I'm just —

HANK: — lurching around this fucking corpse pageant that you think is going to be a party —

MEL: Look, I'm —

HANK: — talking too loud and knocking shit over until they have us booted out?

MEL: Sure!

Pause. Hank regards Mel, coldly.

HANK: Wait a minute. Have you written a script?

MEL: What?

HANK: And are you hoping that I'll look at it, cuz —

MEL: I don't have a script.

HANK: I don't touch that shit.

MEL: I'm practically illiterate.

HANK: You better be.

Pause.

MEL: Hank. I can only pretend to be optimistic up to a point, so are we on or —

HANK: Mel, I swear —

MEL: Don't you want to have some fun?

HANK: Look. I don't know what's going to happen next… but after my shenanigans last night, I know the ending won't be all that pretty. So don't be perceived as being attached to me when the smear campaign gets going. Seriously.

MEL: I'll never ask you again.

Hank drops his head, sighs.

MEL: Just come to the party. I'll help you throw shit around, whatever you want.

HANK: For fuck sake.

MEL: Come on, Hank. (*with finality*) Please.

Long silence. Hank watches Mel. He's perfectly still. Mel waits. Finally, Mel sighs, shifts on his feet. He waits. Hank stares. Mel folds his arms, getting quietly angry.

MEL: Okay?

Hank shakes his head.

MEL: It's gonna be fun.

HANK: Not if I'm there, it isn't.

Pause.

HANK: (*bellows*) Where the hell is the goddamn elevator?

MEL: Oh. They're all out of order. See, there's a sign.

HANK: Well, then why were you standing here, waiting?

MEL: I was waiting for you.

Hank sighs, exits. Mel smiles, watching him go.

Blackout. Hank and Mel enter a blue light.

In disheveled party clothes and somewhat drunk, Hank has an air of melancholy awe as he looks out at us. He sips coffee. Mel's hair is mussed, his tie hanging out of his jacket pocket. He has a bottle of water.

HANK: It doesn't bother you that he's...being held captive here? I mean — in this little pool?

MEL: I know...but he's here now.

Pause. Hank stares at the whale. He nods.

HANK: He certainly is.

MEL: I think seeing him is humbling...for me — he represents, like...evolution and...perfection.

HANK: But he's not a metaphor.

Mel sips his coffee, watches Hank.

HANK: He's a whale. He didn't choose to be here. He's a prisoner.

MEL: Maybe we should go.

HANK: No, no.

Pause. They watch the whale.

MEL: I just thought, since we were passing this way, we could see him... they're conscious breathers, whales.

HANK: What do you mean?

MEL: They decide whether or not to breathe. Like when they sleep, half of their brain stays up to... breathe.

HANK: Okay.

Pause. They watch the whale.

MEL: I went to Europe a few years ago with this guy I used to know. This nut. And we saw an escape artist who could hold his breath for eight minutes.

Hank laughs.

MEL: I swear. We were in a bar in Amsterdam.

Hank chuckles, nods.

MEL: I'm not kidding. We timed him. Exactly eight minutes. He put himself in a trance. He was lying on this tarp. His nose was plugged. His mouth was taped shut. And when he started, he turned red, of course, everything you'd expect. But then he turned dark blue — and — beet purple. Started to swell up. A few of his fingernails split. Tiny veins burst all over and it was like he was sweating blood. We were sure he was going to die and I wanted to say something, but — it was his act, right?

HANK: Right.

MEL: He got really still about six minutes into it. Then someone panicked. She was screaming, *Get it off! Get it off him!* But my friend wouldn't let them take the tape off of his mouth. Not until the eight minutes were up. When the guy finally — finally exhaled — and inhaled again... he made — the most awful sound I've ever heard. The bartender cleaned him up. She touched him as gently as she could... but bruised him all over. Two guys carried him to the back room and that was it ... show was over.

HANK: I love the theatre.

MEL: I decided that it was a reminder not to believe things.

HANK: Uh-huh.

MEL: Also that... um... ideas... are stupid.

Pause. Hank regards Mel, poker-faced.

HANK: You're right out of your mind, aren't you, Mel?

MEL: Since that trip to The Netherlands... I'm a new man, Hank. I am.

Mel nods steadily at Hank. Mel kisses Hank. They consider each other for a moment, as though they have just sampled a spaghetti sauce. They turn and watch the whale. Silence. Hank sips his coffee.

HANK: Been a long time since I've stayed up all night.

MEL: I never sleep.

HANK: I should probably get going.

MEL: Right...I had a good time.

HANK: I have to admit...it was fun.

MEL: So, you wanna get together again or...

HANK: I'm...I think they'll find a way to be rid of me this week, so...I don't know where I'm going.

MEL: Right.

Hank thinks.

HANK: I'll see ya 'round, Mel.

Mel nods. He turns and watches the whale. Hank starts out, stops. He watches Mel for a moment. He obviously has more to say. Mel takes a deep breath, holds it.

Exit Hank.

THE END.

THE RETURNS

THE RETURNS

We hear a low, distant blast from a huge, industrial horn.

We hear a long, slow ocean wave rise and crash on shore.

Lights on Shug Mulls.

He is in a black suit, facing us. Having just landed, his hands are raised and he is looking straight up. His old suit is worn and stained.

The stage is empty except for a megaphone mounted on a pole upstage.

Shug lowers his hands as he notices us watching. He sighs. He shakes his head for a long time, disgusted at the situation.

He removes his jacket, exposing an old white shirt and black suspenders. He rolls up the jacket, tosses it off stage.

Deciding to get it over with, he begins.

SHUG: Welcome to my ... big — um — Play?

He shrugs.

SHUG ... It's a pleasure to almost be here.

A red light grows around Shug.

A gloomy cello plays a few bars as a menacing Shug approaches us, suspiciously.

SHUG: I'll tell ya this much. If we all walked the way we really walk... I'd walk like this.

A bright path of light appears at his feet.

Goofy, bright, discordant piano plays a happy tune.

Shug marches through the light path, out of time with the music, elbows out at the side, rocking from right to left. He smiles broadly and nods crazily, happily as he goes.

When he stops, the light path fades. The red light remains.

A handful of long, menacing notes on the cello. He regards the crowd, bitterly. He shakes his head, disgusted.

Silence.

For a second, he's going to cry. He doesn't. He thinks about the futility.

When he speaks, it's only because he can't think of anything else to do.

SHUG: You know...

He scoffs. Pause. Cuts to the chase.

SHUG: When I — lost consciousness for the last time... my first thought was, "Thank fuck that's over"... all those old bags and strange men hunched around my bed, pissing and moaning, "Oh, Shug, don't leave us." And I had too much morphine and too many tubes in my throat, so there was no way of telling them, "Get out of my room!... this is my big moment, godamnit"... Man, was I glad to be out of there... I could stop wanting things and swallowing my best jabs and trying not to be sick and — best of all — there were no more birds of monotony pecking at the windows of my spongy, beak-hole-filled heart...if you get my drift...do ya get me? Hmm? (*mockingly earnest*) "Yes, we do, Shug. Dead — is an okay way to be. Sure...dead's fine."

He nods and nods at the crowd, a warm smile.

He stops, rolls his head back as he inhales an unwanted breath. He closes his eyes, exhales as sunlight rises and everything turns yellow-gold.

SHUG: We're on the lawn and the baby's shirt says, "This is my first time on this planet." I don't have my glasses so you read it to me. People grin senselessly. Squint over their shades at me. The light cooks us. The baby floats away and sets off a flurry of soft, falsetto voices near the tree. I'm hungry. There's beer in white plastic cups. Scorched beef on the grill. Wine for the bashful. The life-numbing chatter.

He opens his eyes, squints.

He puts on expensive Italian sunglasses.

SHUG: Since the last arduous party, everyone has faded, almost imperceptibly...almost...who's next?...I'm wearing shoes on the grass, so I know I'm one of the old ones...you look the same to me...I watch you sometimes, still — the light in the light...and you find my black shoes and black socks... You have to do everything for me, these days...this long day ...never know when a funeral might break out, you say. And I always laugh. It's all new to me...there's a minute...and another empty minute. A trail of them behind me. You can say they mean something — anything...but the minutes know...it's like that old Norwegian nursery rhyme that goes, "If Life were a little red bus, we'd be in the little red bus exhaust...briefly perfuming the mangled trajectory of demented Time"...or something like that...I think it's from

Norway... I don't really know anything on either side of this, cuz I can't get far enough away to see it all... There's the beauty of it. The pointless beauty. That's all there is. I'm sure of that... They taught us to be ashamed of it...

We keep our plumage on the inside ...

(*mocking sympathy*) Awww... we keep our spikes out and our plumage on the inside — describing and describing what no one else can see... after hilarity, there's only the silence.

He removes his shades. His eyes are closed.

SHUG: I keep forgetting to speak... I remember the number I picked and try to find a good place for a heart attack.

The sunlight bleeds out. The gloom, the red light returns.

Shug opens his eyes.

SHUG: That's the thing... we all picked a number... when you were about five and caught yourself in the mirror or let your mind drift on the water, whatever. For a half a split second you saw through... saw what you would spend years pretending doesn't exist — and you picked a number between one and a hundred and thirty-three. Yes, you did. Yes, you did. We all did. We all Everything... you know? We.ALL... everything ... I'm not trying to hurt you. But you picked a number between one and a hundred and thirty-three. Even though, you probably didn't know what numbers were and the power in them. You picked one and that started the clock ticking... counting down... but in reality — invisible reality two is a way bigger number than sixty-seven and eleven is fucking ridiculous. It's the second last number if you put them in an order that correlates to our surroundings... and what we do ... and how it is.

(*shrugs*) Sorry...I know the number theory doesn't really work here, but this is where the song used to be and I can't find the accordion. And I hate the song...so...it doesn't matter, I'm just supposed to say that it was all...that it was all...like...

He sighs through his nose, thinks.

SHUG: Like this.

He mechanically tap dances the same step over and over on aching feet because there's no other way.

As he dances he stares out, dead-eyed, a machine coming to its inevitable end.

We're glad when he finally stops.

SHUG: All like that...if we had no imagination and never picked a number, we'd live forever...but how fucked would that be, I wonder? (*mockingly, nodding*) "Really fucked, Shug. That's — how much fucked — it would be."

The light returns to normal.

Shug goes to the megaphone mounted on the pole and stands beside it.

SHUG: If everybody talked the way they really talked...I'd talk like this.

He steps behind the megaphone. He has to crouch a little to reach the mouthpiece. He vocalizes through it for about twenty seconds: all ironically poignant squeals, scratchy, inhaling screeches and falsetto screams that recall birds and prehistoric animals.

He stops, steps out from behind the megaphone. Pause. He regards the crowd.

SHUG: Everything I make up is either true already or else becomes true as soon as I say it. Okay, so that's true now...I can only make up true stuff because unlike most in the predicament, I have no imagination...I thought I did, but then...then it was like the tide had taken me as far as it could go...and...Here and Gone —

He mimes, with one angry arm, being pulled back into it.

SHUG ...but then Here again.

Pause. He stares into nothing.

SHUG: Don't know how many times...lost count...ages ago. I know. Not your problem...yet.

He suddenly tenses all of his muscles for a second and then shudders.

SHUG: I've made a lot of bad shit true...and all my life I lied when I didn't have to...the first things I ever showed anyone were the things I wanted to be true. But somehow, that always threw light on the things I hoped no one would ever see... acting is stupid...listen...listen...I can hear the heart pumping again...the tight red fist, clenching and relaxing... too much of this is automatic...what was I thinking — (*quietly*) for?

Blackout. Lights up. A distant 1920s recording of a love song plays backwards.

SHUG: The sun is gone. There's a voice singing backwards in my head. Medication bonus. There's someone outside going through the cans in the garbage. Shrapnel clangs in the shopping cart. It's the night's bell...worn out alarm...we're up here, safe as latex. The walls knock and creak with electric heat ...I've been taking old pills prescribed to me a few years ago. Rewiring my brain, poking Death with a stick...see if it tries to hook me. But even if it does, I'll come surfacing, slowly, out of the pool of tar...and go again... (*nodding*) right?

The red light returns. Shug regards the audience bitterly.

SHUG: You're dead.

Blackout. Lights up.

Blackout. Bright, yellow-gold lights. The music fades.

Shug is wearing his shades, facing us.

SHUG: I'm starting to forget...I reach back for things and there's nothing...and of course, I can't imagine...so.

Blackout. Lights up.

SHUG: I couldn't remember my name once...how do you forget your own name?...Especially a name like Shug...Shug Mulls. Sugar Mulls. Sugar. Cuz I was sweet, apparently. As a baby, I assume. Shug Mulls. Sounds made-up, cuz it is. They all are...wow...time isn't a concept anymore...it has me...I'm Not.

Blackout. Lights up.

SHUG: Not Ever and Never Was...What's going to happen down the road?...Further down the road...I won't let you take care of me.

He removes his glasses. Pause. His eyes are closed.

SHUG: I forget all the shit I hate, too...so my blood pressure is down...you say 'That's good, Shug'...Well, why? Good for you, maybe...but what's the point for me...I wondered...

Blackout.

SHUG: I still wonder.

Lights up.

SHUG: Why...

Blackout. Lights. The shades are gone. There is a lawn chair downstage.

SHUG: They hand the baby over and she coos at me, grinning and drooling — and the world unravels endlessly before her and you read her shirt to me. It says, "This is my first time on this planet." I don't get it. I want food. Something made by one of my family. I hand the toothless goddess to some cousin and I make my way. White paper tablecloth waving at flies. Nameless children run past howling, nut brown and barefoot. *Shug!*

He sits.

SHUG: I remember the number. I put the plate in the grass and decide on the lawn chair. You wanna be sitting down when the heart stops. It's always better sitting...isn't it?

He nods, then shakes his head. He stands.

SHUG: Thanks for coming to my big comedy show.

Silence. He shades his eyes and looks to the back of the house. Now he's mad. He looks up at the booth.

SHUG: Put the lights out... PUT THE FUCKING LIGHTS OUT!

SFX: a distant blast from a huge, industrial sounding horn.

SHUG: Oh, for fuck sake!

SFX: A wave.

Shug considers the approaching wall of water, raises his hands, readies himself as the light grows brighter and brighter.

Blackout as the wave crashes.

SFX: another blast from the industrial horn that sounded at the beginning.

THE END.

ABOUT THE PLAYWRIGHT

ED MACDONALD was born and raised on Cape Breton Island. He grew up in the theatre—writing, directing, and acting—until moving on to screenwriting. He has won three Gemini Awards for his work in television and has been nominated many times. He has won the The Golden Sheaf and The Writer's Guild of Canada Award. In 2005, he was nominated for the New York Innovative Theatre Award. His debut novel, *Spat the Dummy,* was published by Anvil Press in 2010, and his follow-up novel, *Atomic Storybook,* (Anvil) will be released in the spring of 2013. Ed lives in Toronto.